I0016026

WordPerfect® 6.1 for Windows™ Instant Reference

Second Edition

Alan Simpson

toExcel

San Jose New York Lincoln Shanghai

WordPerfect® 6.1 for Windows™ Instant Reference 2.

For information address:
toExcel
165 West 95th Street, Suite B-N
New York, NY 10025
www.toExcel.com

This edition published by arrangement with toExcel,
a strategic unit of Kaleidoscope Software, Inc.
Marca registrada
toExcel
New York, NY

ISBN: 1583482121

Library of Congress Catalog Card Number: 99-61424

Printed in the United States of America

0 9 8 7 6 5 4 3 2 1

To Susan, Ashley, and Alec

Acknowledgments

Every book is a team effort, and this one is certainly no exception. The skills, talents, and hard work of many people brought this book from the idea stage into your hands.

On the publishing side the following people were instrumental in creating this book: Sarah Wadsworth, developmental editor; Michelle Nance and Kris Vanberg-Wolff, editors; Sheila Dienes, Erik Ingenito, and Tanya Strub, technical editors; Carolina Montilla, production editor; Sarah Lemas, production coordinator; Lisa Jaffe, production artist; Cuong Le, screen graphics; Aldo X. Bermudez, graphics file manager; and Stephanie Hollier, desktop publishing specialist.

On the authorial side, the talented writers Elizabeth Olson and Martha Mellor provided most of the material in this book; Martha Mellor miraculously managed to put it all together.

Thanks to Bill Gladstone and Matt Wagner of Waterside Production for handling business matters.

Susan, Ashley, and Alec provided love, support, sustenance, comfort, and lots of patience.

Table of Contents

Introduction
xvii

Index

Introduction

WordPerfect Corporation has taken all the best features of the graphical user interface and incorporated them beautifully into their version 6.1 of the now-legendary WordPerfect word processing program. Both beginners and old hands alike will appreciate the intuitive, interactive means of creating and editing documents that WordPerfect 6.1 for Windows brings to the personal computer.

WHO SHOULD READ THIS BOOK

This book is designed for WordPerfect users who are on the go. Its portable yet comprehensive format provides ready access to all those big features and little details that are so easily forgotten. Of course, the compact size does not allow for lengthy tutorials about every feature, so if you're new to WordPerfect for Windows, you may want to back this book up with a more comprehensive tutorial, such as *Mastering WordPerfect 6.1 for Windows Special Edition*, also published by SYBEX.

HOW TO USE THIS BOOK

This book is organized as an encyclopedic reference, with topics arranged alphabetically. Each reference section includes (as appropriate):

- A general description of the feature
- Step-by-step instructions for the use of the feature
- Notes providing additional usage tips and suggestions
- Cross-references to related topics and features

To speed things along, we often present a series of menu selections with an arrow (➤) separating each option and the optional letter choice for each option underlined. If the command has a shortcut key sequence, we'll present it in parentheses, like this:

Choose Format ➤ Margins (Ctrl+F8).

You can use any of the usual Windows techniques—the mouse, the arrow keys, or the keyboard—for choosing menu options. If you are not already familiar with these techniques, perhaps your best starting point would be to refer to the "Mouse" and "Menus" sections in this book.

NEW FEATURES IN 6.1

WordPerfect for Windows version 6.0 was a substantial upgrade to version 5.2, offering a host of new and improved features. Word-Perfect for Windows version 6.1 added many new wrinkles to version 6.0, including several new features, some subtle changes, and many performance improvements. In this book, we've marked features introduced in version 6.1 with a special heading like this:

In cases where the changes between version 6.0 and 6.1 are mainly cosmetic, we've described only the most up-to-date version 6.1 feature, and have not marked the heading in any special way.

INSTALLING AND STARTING
WORDPERFECT FOR WINDOWS

See the Install entry in this book for details about installing and starting WordPerfect for Windows.

This book includes some information on Windows 95 made public by Microsoft as of 11/14/94. Since this information was made public before the release of the product, we encourage you to visit your local bookstore at that time for updated books on Windows 95.

If you have a modem or access to the Internet, you can always get up-to-the-minute information on Windows 95 direct from Microsoft on WinNews:

On CompuServe:	GO WINNEWS
On the Internet:	ftp://ftp.microsoft.com/PerO p.Sys/Win_News/Chicago
	http://www.microsoft.com
On AOL:	keyword WINNEWS
On Prodigy:	jumpword WINNEWS
On Genie	WINNEWS file area on Windows RTC

You can also subscribe to Microsoft's WinNews electronic newsletter by sending Internet email to cnews@microsoft.nwnet.com and putting the words SUBSCRIBE WINNEWS in the text of the email.

THE WORDPERFECT DOCUMENT WINDOW

The graphic on the next page shows the WordPerfect window with all of its "tools" visible. For more information about the tools shown, please see the following entries in this book: Toolbar, Codes, Cursor, Document Window, Menus, Mouse, Power Bar, Reveal Codes, Ruler, and Status Bar.

WORDPERFECT KEYBOARDS

In this book, we assume that you will be using the default WPWin 6.1 Keyboard. *If you have any problems duplicating the instructions presented in this book, a keyboard other than the WordPerfect for Windows 6.1 keyboard may be in use.* To switch back to the default keyboard:

1. Choose Edit ➤ Preferences and double-click Keyboard.

2. Highlight WPWin 6.1 Keyboard> and choose Select.

3. Choose Close.

The WPWin 6.1 keystrokes will then work properly, and the pull-down menus will show the appropriate shortcut keys.

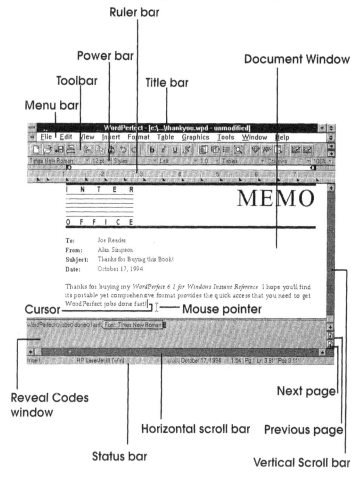

WordPerfect 6.1's Hottest New Features

The section below summarizes some of the new and modified features in WordPerfect for Windows version 6.1. You can find additional information about each topic under the appropriate heading in the book.

Documents and Files

Open As Copy Lets you open a read-only copy of a document, then use the copy as a model for a new document or as a way to view multiple parts of the same document.

Password Protection Allows you to choose either of two methods for protecting files with passwords.

Formatting and Styles

Drop Cap Create glamorous drop caps at the start of any paragraph, instantly and painlessly. Choose from more than a dozen predefined styles, or customize your own.

Make It Fit Expert Reformat margins, fonts, and line spacing in your document to fit on a specified number of pages.

QuickFormat Quickly copy formatting codes from one paragraph to another. If you change the style in one place, WordPerfect updates the same style automatically in the rest of the document.

Undo and Redo WordPerfect can remember up to 300 of your most recent editing and formatting changes. You can then undo or redo your changes one-by-one or in a big chunk.

Graphics

Drag To Create Lets you insert images and size any graphics box by clicking and dragging in your document.

Draw, Chart, and TextArt These mini-applications are better, faster, and easier to use than ever.

Help

Help Now features an expanded How Do I section, an Examples index, and Coaches you can select while you are in Help.

QuickStart Coach Provides a quick introduction to WordPerfect features. This Coach appears the first time you run WordPerfect and whenever you choose Help ➤ Coaches ➤ QuickStart ➤ OK.

Upgrade Expert Helps upgraders and new users get up to speed quickly. Use the Upgrade Expert to perform tasks automatically or to get more information about those tasks.

Information Sharing

Object Exchange (OBEX) Provides another way to share data with other users across a network, phone line, or other communication service. Requires PerfectOffice or other OBEX-enabled applications such as Quattro Pro and Paradox.

Object Linking and Embedding (OLE 2) Object Linking and Embedding makes it easy to put data created by other Windows applications into your WordPerfect documents, and to view, play back, or edit that data without leaving WordPerfect. New OLE 2 support offers in-place editing, drag-and-drop across programs and document windows, and linking or embedding of any OLE object.

Universal Naming Conventions (UNC) For network users, WordPerfect supports Novell and UNC anywhere a path and file name are allowed.

Integration with Perfect Office and Other Novell Applications

Common User Interface WordPerfect 6.1 is part of an integrated suite of applications called PerfectOffice. Many changes were made to ensure compatibility among applications in the suite, including: A shared interface with PerfectOffice 3.0, for a similar "look and feel" among all applications in the suite; "PerfectFit" technology, which allows Novell applications to share many features and capabilities, including a common macro language; and "PerfectScript," a macro language that lets you create automated processes for working with multiple applications such as WordPerfect and Quattro Pro.

Macros

Template Macros   Macros stored on disk and macros stored in templates are now handled separately in version 6.1. This makes it easier to choose which macros to play, record, and edit.

Screen/Interface

Button Bar and Power Bar   The button bar is now called a toolbar. Both the toolbar and power bar were redesigned.

Cut And Paste   WordPerfect automatically adds or deletes spaces where needed when you cut, paste, or drag and drop words and phrases.

Menus   The Layout menu was renamed to Format, the Preferences option on the File menu was moved to the Edit menu, and the Find and Replace options on the Edit menu were combined into a single Edit ➤ Find And Replace option.

Paste Simple   When you use Paste Simple (Ctrl+Shift+V) to paste text from the Clipboard into your document, the pasted text will have the same appearance as the paragraph you're pasting it into (rather than its original appearance).

QuickSelect Text   With QuickSelect, you can double-click, triple-click, or quadruple-click to select a chunk of text; then hold down the Shift key while clicking (or dragging to) the next or previous chunk of same-sized text.

Tables and Charts

Charts Created Automatically   You can create a chart from a table, then have WordPerfect update the chart automatically whenever you change numbers or formulas in the table.

Row/Column Indicators   Spreadsheet-like row and column indicators make it easier to select rows, columns, or the entire table.

Size To Fit   Instantly resize a column or columns to fit the text they contain. You'll love this one!

Table Expert   Apply professionally-designed table formats with just a few clicks of your mouse.

Templates

Templates and Document Experts   WordPerfect comes with more than fifty document templates that make it easy to create and fill in documents such as brochures, letters, calendars, newsletters, and fax cover sheets. Templates have been revamped since WordPerfect 6.0 and work somewhat differently.

Writing Tools

Find And Replace   The separate Find and Replace features have been combined into a single menu option (Edit ➤ Find And Replace). You can now find and replace word forms. For instance, replace *drive, drove*, **or** *driven*, **with** *run, ran*, **or** *run,* **respectively.**

Grammatik 6   Grammatik is easier to use. It also features a parts-of-speech and parse-tree viewer, and enhanced document statistics that provide a clearer idea of your document's readability.

QuickCorrect   As you type, QuickCorrect will instantly fix misspelled words, substitute abbreviations with expanded text, correct certain capitalization and spacing errors, and replace straight quotation marks with balanced "SmartQuotes."

Spell Checker   The Spell Checker (formerly named Speller) has been overhauled. It can even look up words in, and automatically enter words into, the QuickCorrect dictionary while you're spell checking.

Thesaurus   Thesaurus now lets you look up words using any form. For instance, you can highlight the word *drive, drove,* or *driven* and find a list of synonyms that include *motor, pilot, propel, steer,* and *chase.*

ABBREVIATIONS

It is sometimes easier to type an abbreviation or select it from a menu and have WordPerfect expand it for you than it is to type the whole word each time.

To Create an Abbreviation

1. Select the text you want to abbreviate.

2. Choose Insert ➤ Abbreviations, then choose Create from the Abbreviations dialog box.

3. Type an abbreviation for the selected text. The name is case-sensitive.

4. Choose OK, then choose Close to return to the document window.

To Expand an Abbreviation

Once you've set up an abbreviation, proceed as follows to insert the expanded form into your document:

1. Type the abbreviation (*exactly* as you typed it when creating the abbreviation) and place the cursor on the abbreviated text.

2. Press Ctrl+A.

If you prefer to expand an abbreviation without typing it first, follow these steps:

1. Position the cursor where you want the full text to appear.

2. Choose Insert ➤ Abbreviations to open the Abbreviations dialog box.

3. Double-click the abbreviation you want to expand, or highlight it and choose Expand.

To Replace an Abbreviation with a New Selection

1. Select the text that should replace the abbreviation when you expand it later.

2. Choose Insert ➤ Abbreviations and highlight the abbreviation you want to change.

3. Choose Replace, answer Yes when asked for comfirmation, and choose Close to return to your document.

To Rename an Abbreviation

1. Choose Insert ➤ Abbreviations and highlight the abbreviation you want to rename.

2. Choose Rename, and type the new abbreviation.

3. Choose OK, then choose Close.

To Delete an Abbreviation

1. Choose Insert ➤ Abbreviations and highlight the abbreviation you want to delete.

2. Choose Delete, answer Yes when asked for confirmation, and choose Close to return to your document.

To Copy an Abbreviation to Another Template

1. Choose Insert ➤ Abbreviations.

2. Choose Copy. The Copy Abbreviation dialog box opens.

3. Select the template to copy from, the abbreviation you want to copy, and the template you want to copy to. Choose Copy.

NOTES You can also use Find And Replace to expand abbreviated text, and use the QuickCorrect feature to expand text as you type.

👁 **SEE ALSO** *QuickCorrect, Replace, Template*

ADVANCE

Use Advance to move text to an exact horizontal and vertical position relative to the cursor or relative to the left and top edges of the page. Advance is often used to position the cursor in pre-printed forms.

To Position Text on the Page

1. Move the cursor to the page where you want to advance the text. If you want to advance text relative to the cursor position, place the cursor where you want the advance to begin.

2. Choose Format ➤ Typesetting ➤ Advance.

3. Choose a horizontal positioning method. Your options are None (no horizontal change in position), Left From Insertion Point, Right From Insertion Point, and From Left Edge Of Page.

4. For horizontal positions other than None, specify the Horizontal Distance to advance.

5. Choose a vertical position. Your options are None (no vertical change in position), Up From Insertion Point, Down From Insertion Point, and From Top Of Page.

6. For vertical positions other than None, specify the Vertical Distance to advance.

7. If you chose From Top Of Page, you can select or deselect Text Above Position. This option positions text above (when selected) or below (when deselected) the specified position.

8. Choose OK.

 NOTES To return the cursor to the original position, repeat the steps above, but advance in opposite directions by the same distance.

You can't advance text past a page break onto another page, nor can you advance from within a table or columns to above the table or columns.

When using Advance for pre-printed forms, you might find it works best to choose Format ➤ Typesetting ➤ Word/Letterspacing and select Baseline Placement For Typesetting. You may also want to enter a fixed line height (Format ➤ Line ➤ Height ➤ Fixed).

👁 **SEE ALSO** *Line Height, Typesetting, Units of Measure*

APPEND

The Append command adds selected text or graphics to the existing contents of the Clipboard.

To Add Elements to the Clipboard

1. Select the desired text.

2. Choose Edit ➤ Append.

The Append command is not available unless you've already put something on the Clipboard with Edit ➤ Copy or Edit ➤ Cut. The appended material remains on the Clipboard until you replace it with Cut or Copy or exit Windows.

NOTES   All attributes of the appended text, such as boldface or italics, are preserved when appended to the Clipboard.

SEE ALSO   *Combine Documents; Cut, Copy, and Paste; Selecting Text*

BAR CODE

Add POSTNET Bar Codes to mailing addresses to speed up and ensure accurate delivery of your mail.

To Insert a POSTNET Bar Code in a Document

1. Position the cursor where you want the POSTNET Bar Code to appear. Most likely, this will be just above or below the mailing address on a label or envelope.

2. Choose Insert ➤ Other ➤ Bar Code.

3. Enter a 5-digit Zip Code (e.g., 92123), 9-digit Zip+4 Code (e.g., 92123-0987), or 11-digit Delivery Point Bar Code (e.g.,92123-0987-21).

4. Choose OK.

NOTES   You can also add POSTNET Bar Codes when defining an envelope via Format ➤ Envelope. See the Envelope entry.

SEE ALSO   *Envelope, Labels, Merge Operations, Paper Size*

BINDING/DUPLEX

The Binding/Duplex command shifts text on the page to provide extra space for binding and to activate duplex (two-sided) printing. Use it if you're planning to bind a document that's printed on both sides of the paper.

To Set a Binding Edge or Duplex Printing

1.   Select Format ➤ Page ➤ Binding/Duplex.

2.   Choose a binding edge (Left, Right, Top, or Bottom).

3.   Specify the Amount of space to leave at the binding edge. To remove the binding offset, enter zero (0).

4.   If your printer supports duplexing (printing on both sides of the page), you can choose one of the Duplexing options below:

Off   No duplexing. (Useful if you don't want duplexing or if your printer can't duplex.)

From Short Edge   Use when binding on the short side of a page (like a flip chart). This prints text upside down on the back side of a page.

From Long Edge   Use when binding the long edge of a page (like a book).

5.   Choose OK.

NOTES   It's best to set the binding options before you create your document.

A Left binding offset shifts text to the right on odd-numbered pages and to the left on even-numbered pages. A Top binding offset shifts text down on odd-numbered pages and up on even-numbered pages.

The binding offset is added to the inside margin (the margin on the edge that will be bound) and subtracted from the outside margin (the margin on the edge opposite the bound edge).

To get even margins, enter an offset value that's half of what you actually intend and add the same amount to both margins (see *Example*).

To bind a document that's printed on one side only, choose Fo_r_mat ➤ P_a_ragraph ➤ _F_ormat and specify a _L_eft Margin Adjustment instead of using the Binding feature.

If your printer doesn't support duplex printing, you can print on both sides of the paper by using _F_ile ➤ _P_rint ➤ _O_ptions ➤ Print _O_dd/Even Pages. Print odd pages first, then reload the odd pages into the printer to print the even pages on the back side.

EXAMPLE   For a ½-inch binding offset, binding at the left edge, and 1-inch left and right margins, set the binding offset to 0.25 inch and increase the left and right margins to 1.25 inches.

 **SEE ALSO**   *Margins, Paper Size, Paragraph, Print, Units of Measure*

BOOKLETS AND PAMPHLETS

A booklet typically consists of 8.5×11 (or larger) sheets of paper folded in half and stapled on the fold. A pamphlet is basically the same thing, but folded lengthwise to make a tall, thin, multi-page document that fits in your pocket. This section explains how to set up booklets and pamphlets.

To Set Up a Booklet or Pamphlet

1. Optionally, choose View ➤ Two Page to view your document.

2. Move the cursor to the top of the document (press Ctrl+Home twice). Choose Format ➤ Page ➤ Paper Size, and highlight the paper definition you want. For a standard pamphlet, choose Letter size (8.5×11). For a booklet, choose Letter Landscape (or another landscape definition). Choose Select.

3. Choose Format ➤ Page ➤ Subdivide Page, set Number of Columns to 2, and choose OK.

4. If you want smaller margins on each page, use Format ➤ Margins to reduce the margins (for example, to .5 inches all around).

5. Optionally, add borders around the pages by choosing Format ➤ Page ➤ Border/Fill. Select a Border Style and choose OK.

6. Type your document normally. If necessary, insert hard page breaks (Ctrl+↵) to begin new pages.

To Print a Booklet or Pamphlet (Duplex Printer)

1. If your printer supports duplex printing, move the cursor to the top of the document (press Ctrl+Home), and choose Format ➤ Page ➤ Binding/Duplex. Set Duplexing to From Short Edge (for a booklet) or From Long Edge (for a pamphlet). Choose OK.

2. Choose File ➤ Print ➤ Options, select Booklet Printing, and choose OK.

3. Choose Print to start printing.

When printing finishes, fold the pages in half and staple them at the fold.

To Print a Booklet or Pamphlet (Non-Duplex Printer)

If you don't have a duplex printer, try these steps to print a booklet or pamphlet:

1. Make sure you follow steps 1–6 at the start of this entry to define your paper size and page subdivision. Then move the cursor to the bottom of the document (press Ctrl+End). If the number of the last page is not evenly divisible by 4, press Ctrl+↵ to insert blank pages until it is. For example, the last page in your document should be 8, 12, 16, 20, or so forth, as indicated by the Pg prompt in the status bar.

2. Choose File ➤ Print ➤ Options ➤ Booklet Printing ➤ Print Odd/Even Page ➤ Odd ➤ OK ➤ Print.

3. After the pages are printed, remove them but do not rotate them. Instead, open the paper tray, and put the page that's on the top of the stack face down into the paper tray, until all the pages are back in the printer. You want Page 1 to be face down, on the top of that stack, since the next print pass will start printing at page 2.

4. Choose File ➤ Print ➤ Options ➤ Booklet Printing ➤ Print Odd/Even Page ➤ Even ➤ OK ➤ Print.

After the pages are printed, you should be able to reverse the order of the pages once again, then staple in the center to create the booklet.

NOTES   You may need a stapler with an exceptionally long reach to staple the booklet pages together. Check your local stationery or office supply store. I've had success with the "Foot Long Adjustable Stapler" available from Paper Direct at (800)A-PAPERS.

 **SEE ALSO**   *Binding/Duplex, Paper Size, Print*

BOOKMARK

WordPerfect's bookmark feature lets you insert a *bookmark* as a placeholder in text so that you can locate that place again quickly. There are two kinds of bookmarks: QuickMark bookmarks and named bookmarks. Each document can have only one QuickMark bookmark, but as many named bookmarks as you want.

To Create a QuickMark Bookmark

1. Position the cursor where you want to set the QuickMark.
2. Press Ctrl+Shift+Q.

To Return the Cursor to a QuickMark Bookmark

• Press Ctrl+Q.

To Set QuickMarks Automatically

1. Choose Edit ➤ Preferences and double-click Environment.
2. Select (check) Set QuickMark On Save.
3. Choose OK, then choose Close.

This will automatically set a QuickMark at the cursor position whenever you close any document.

To Use Named Bookmarks in a Document

1. If you want to add a new bookmark or move an existing bookmark, position the cursor where you want the book-mark. If you want to select text at the bookmark when you jump back to it later, select the text you'll want to jump to later.

2. Choose Insert ➤ Bookmark. You now have several choices:

- To *create a new bookmark*, choose Create, type a unique name for your bookmark, and choose OK. Or, to set a QuickMark bookmark, choose Set QuickMark.

- To *return to an existing bookmark,* highlight its name and choose Go To. To return to a bookmark created with se-lected text, highlight the bookmark's name and choose Go To & Select. To return to a QuickMark bookmark, choose Find QuickMark.

- To *delete a bookmark*, highlight its name, then choose Delete and answer Yes when prompted. (You can also delete a bookmark by deleting its [Bookmark] code in Reveal Codes.)

- To *move a bookmark* to the current cursor location in your document, highlight the bookmark's name and choose Move.

- To *rename a bookmark,* highlight the bookmark, choose Rename, edit the name, and choose OK.

3. Choose Close, if necessary, to return to the document window.

NOTES   You can get to the Bookmark dialog box quickly by double-clicking any [Bookmark] code in Reveal Codes. The Tem-plate feature (File ➤ New) uses numbered bookmarks (e.g., 1, 2, 3…) to substitute text in documents created from certain templates. Therefore, you should avoid moving, deleting, or renaming num-bered bookmarks, and you should not use numbers for your own bookmark names. Otherwise, the results may be unpredictable.

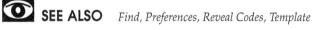 **SEE ALSO**   *Find, Preferences, Reveal Codes, Template*

BULLETS AND NUMBERS

The Bullets and Numbers feature lets you type a list in which items are marked automatically with bullets, numbers, roman numerals, or letters.

To Type a Bulleted or Numbered List

1. Position the cursor where you want the list to begin.

2. Choose Insert ➤ Bullets & Numbers.

3. In the Styles list, highlight the character you want to put at the start of the item. (If you choose a number, roman numeral, or letter, WordPerfect will increment markers automatically when you add a list item and will decrement markers when you delete an item.)

4. If you want a new bullet or number to appear automatically when you press ⏎, select New Bullet Or Number On ENTER.

5. If necessary, select Starting Value and enter a starting number and Paragraph Level for the first marked item.

6. Choose OK.

7. Type the text of the item and press ⏎. (If you didn't select New Bullet Or Number On ENTER in step 4, you can add a blank line by pressing ⏎ a second time.)

To type the remaining items in the list, use either of the methods below:

- If you selected New Bullet Or Number on ENTER in step 4 above, type the next item and press ⏎. Repeat this step until you've typed all the items. When you're done, choose Insert ➤ Bullets & Numbers, select <None> in the Styles list, and choose OK. Or, when the last item marker appears on its own line, press Backspace to delete the marker and turn off the bullets or numbering.

- If you didn't select New Bullet Or Number On ENTER in step 4, press Ctrl+Shift+B, type the next item, and press ↵ (twice if you want a blank line between items). Repeat this step until you've typed all the items.

NOTES   To change the style of bulleted or numbered items in a list created with this feature, choose Insert ➤ Bullets & Numbers. Highlight the style you want to change and choose Edit. Edit the style as you would any style, then choose OK twice.

If you selected New Bullet Or Number On ENTER in step 4 and want to add blank lines between items, position the cursor just above the list, or select all the items in the list. Choose Format ➤ Paragraph ➤ Format ➤ Spacing Between Paragraphs, enter a Spacing greater than 1, and choose OK. For example, a line spacing of 2 puts one blank line between entries.

SEE ALSO   *Line Spacing, List, Outline, Styles*

CANCEL

Cancel is WordPerfect's universal "get me out of trouble" feature. Use it to back out of menu choices, cancel any operation that displays a prompt or menu, or stop a macro or merge operation before it finishes.

To Cancel the Current Operation

Cancel an operation in any of the following ways:

- Choose Cancel from a dialog box.
- Double-click the Control-menu box of a dialog box you want to back out of.

- Click the document window outside an open menu you want to cancel.

- Using the keyboard, press Escape (Esc).

NOTES You may need to cancel more than once when backing out of menus to reach the document window.

SEE ALSO *Document Window, Exit, Undelete, Undo/Redo*

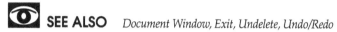

CENTER

You can center text horizontally between margins or within columns.

To Center One Line of Text

1. Position the cursor where you want to center new text or at the beginning of an existing line of text.

2. Choose Format ➤ Line ➤ Center (Shift+F7). WordPerfect will center the text between the margins.

3. If you want dot leaders, repeat step 2.

4. If you are centering new text, type the new text and press ↵.

To Center Large Sections of Text

1. Position the cursor above the text to be centered, or select a block of text.

2. Choose Format ➤ Justification ➤ Center, or press Ctrl+E.

The text will be centered horizontally until the next justification code or until the end of the document.

NOTES   To center text vertically (top to bottom) on the page, see *Center Page*.

SEE ALSO   *Center Page, Justification, Page Breaks, Selecting Text, Tabs*

CENTER PAGE

This command centers all text vertically on the page between the top and bottom margins.

To Center Text Vertically

1. Position the cursor at the top of the page of text to be centered.

2. Choose Format ➤ Page ➤ Center.

3. Choose a centering option (Current Page, Current And Subsequent Pages, or No Centering).

4. Choose OK.

NOTES   If additional text follows the text to be centered vertically (for example, a document that follows a centered title page), move the cursor to the end of the vertically centered text and insert a hard page break (Ctrl+↵ or Ctrl+Shift+↵).

SEE ALSO   *Center, Page Breaks*

CHARACTERS

WordPerfect lets you enter hundreds of characters that you can't otherwise type on your keyboard. These include mathematical, scientific, multinational, typographic, and iconic symbols, as well as letters for several foreign-language alphabets.

To Insert a Special Character

1. Position the cursor where you want the special character to appear.

2. Press Ctrl+W or choose Insert ➤ Character.

3. Do either of the following:

- Choose a character set from the Character Set pop-up list button, then click on the character you want in the Characters list.

- Choose Number and type the character set number, a comma, and the character number. For example, choose Number and type **5,0** for the heart character in the Iconic Symbols character set.

4. To insert the character and return to your document, choose Insert And Close. To insert the character and remain in the WordPerfect Characters dialog box, choose Insert. (If you choose Insert, you can repeat steps 3–4 as needed; then choose Close to return to the document window.)

 **SEE ALSO** *Font, Overstrike*

Chart 17

CHART

WordPerfect has a built-in charting package that can produce pie, bar, line, area, scatter, and hi-lo charts in many different formats. You can enter data into the Chart application's Datasheet window, or you can chart data that's stored in a table in your document. Finished charts are placed into graphics boxes in your document.

Chart was improved significantly for WordPerfect version 6.1.

To Create a Chart

1. Position your cursor as follows:

   • To chart an entire table that's in your document, put the cursor anywhere in the table.

   • To chart specific cells, rows, and columns in the table, select them.

   • To enter data for the chart manually, put the cursor where you want the chart to appear, outside of any tables.

2. Choose Graphics ➤ Chart, or click the Chart button in the WordPerfect or Tables toolbar. The Chart Editor will open for in- place editing in your document. If you did not put the cursor in a table in step 1, the screen will include a Datasheet window, as illustrated in Figure 1. If you did put the cursor in a table, that Datasheet window won't appear (it's not needed, since the table already specifies the data to be charted).

3. If you started from a table in step 1, skip to step 4 now. Otherwise, click the Datasheet window, size and position it as you would any window, and update its cells with the data you want to chart. The basic techniques are the same as for changing tables. You can also use these techniques:

   • To *clear all the data* in the table, choose Edit ➤ Clear All or press Ctrl+Shift+F4, then choose Yes.

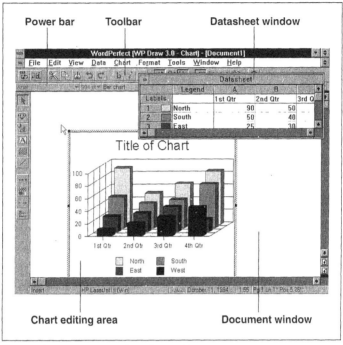

Figure 1: The WordPerfect Chart Editor

- To *select (highlight) columns or rows* in the table, click on
  the label for the column or row, or drag the mouse
  through the column or row labels to select several at
  once. (You can also hold down the Shift key and press
  an arrow key to select columns, rows, or cells.)

- To *insert and delete columns or rows* in the table, select the
  column or row. Then choose Edit ➤ Insert or Edit ➤ Delete, as appropriate.

- To *cut or copy and paste* data, position the cursor in
  a cell or select cells, rows, or columns. Choose Edit
  then Cut or Copy. Position the cursor where you
  want to paste the data. Choose Edit, then Paste or
  Paste Transposed. (Paste Transposed converts row
  data to column data and vice versa.)

Chart 19

- To *go to a specific cell*, choose Edit ➤ Go To Cell or press Ctrl+G, specify the cell address, and choose OK.

- *To control the Datasheet window's appearance*, or to include or exclude a row or column from the Datasheet, choose options from the Data menu.

- To *change labels for the legend*, type the labels in the Legend column of the Datasheet window, in the row for whatever series the label describes.

- To *hide or show the Datasheet window*, choose View ➤ Datasheet, or click on the View Datasheet button on the toolbar.

4. Use any of the techniques below to customize the appearance of the chart:

- To *choose a chart type*, click the Data Chart Types button in the power bar, then choose a chart type. Or, choose Chart ➤ Type or Chart ➤ Gallery and select appropriate chart types.

- To *customize a data series*, choose Chart ➤ Series and use the Next or Previous button to locate the series you want to change. Or, right-click the series you want to change and choose Edit Series from the QuickMenu.

- To *control chart redrawing*, choose options from the View menu. View ➤ Auto Redraw (or the Auto Redraw button in the toolbar) turns automatic redrawing on or off. When Auto Redraw is off (unchecked), you must choose View ➤ Redraw (or press Ctrl+F3 or click the Redraw button in the toolbar) to redraw the chart with your latest changes.

- To *customize the chart's layout*, series axes, grid and tick marks, frame, perspective, titles, legend, or labels, choose options from the Chart menu. Or, right-click the area you want to format and choose an appropriate option from the QuickMenu. You can also use buttons in the toolbar and power bar.

- To *get help with charting*, choose Help ➤ How Do I, then click *Charts* and select topics as needed.

5. When you're finished creating the chart, click in the document editing area outside the chart, or click the Close button in the toolbar. If necessary, deselect the chart's graphics box by clicking outside the box again.

To Edit an Existing Chart

- In the document window, double-click the chart's graphics box.

- Or right-click the box and choose Chart Object. Then, if you want to edit the chart in-place (without leaving the WordPerfect document window), choose Edit. If you want to edit the chart in a separate application window, choose Open.

- When you're ready to return to the document window, click the Close button in the toolbar. Or, click in the Word-Perfect document window outside the chart box (if you were editing in place), or choose File ➤ Exit And Return To Document (if you were editing in a separate application window). If necessary, click outside the chart box again to deselect it.

To Annotate a Chart in the Draw Package

- In the document window, right-click the chart box and choose Chart Object ➤ Annotate from the QuickMenu.

- Or, if you are in the Chart Editor already, right-click an empty area of the chart and choose Annotate from the QuickMenu.

NOTES The easiest way to learn the Chart package is to use the guidelines given above and then experiment.

You can move the mouse pointer to most buttons in the Chart toolbar or power bar to find out what the buttons are for. A description of the button will appear near the mouse pointer.

Once created, a chart box can be sized, captioned, positioned, and edited in the same way as any normal graphics box.

SEE ALSO *Draw, Graphics and Graphics Boxes, Object Linking and Embedding, Spreadsheet/Database Import and Link, Tables*

CODES

Codes are used to control formatting in WordPerfect. Normally these are hidden, unless you turn on the Reveal Codes window (View ➤ Reveal Codes or Alt+F3). See the Reveal Codes entry for details about using the Reveal Codes window.

NOTES *Single codes* affect all text beyond them, up to another single code that changes the setting. *Paired codes* affect only the text between the codes.

In the example below, [Ln Spacing:2.0] is a single code that double-spaces all text below it (up to the next [Ln Spacing] code, if any). The [Italc] codes are paired codes that italicize the *Getting Started* text between the codes.

[Ln Spacing:2.0][Italc]*Getting Started* [Italc]: To start the

engine, insert the key and turn it to the right

Codes are inserted automatically when you press a formatting key (such as Tab or ↵), or when you choose formatting options from the menus. To find out what a code is for, turn on Reveal Codes (Alt+F3) and point to the code with your mouse. A description of the code will appear in the WordPerfect title bar.

You can find and replace *specific codes* (such as a certain font) or *general codes* (such as any type of Tab).

SEE ALSO *Find, Initial Codes Style, Initial Font, Replace, Reveal Codes, Styles*

COLUMNS

The Columns command lets you format text and graphics into multiple columns.

To Define Columns

1.   Move the cursor to where the columns should begin.

2.   Choose Format ➤ Columns ➤ Define, double-click the Columns Define button in the power bar, or right-click the ruler bar and choose Columns. Or, click the Columns Define button in the power bar and choose Define.

3.   Choose Columns and specify the number of columns you want (between 2 and 24, inclusive).

4.   Choose one of the following types of columns:

Newspaper   "Snaking" columns, in which text ends at the bottom of one column and resumes at the top of the next.

Balanced Newspaper   "Snaking" text is equally distributed between columns.

Parallel   Each column is printed independently, side-by-side on a page; each column's text carries over to the next page.

Parallel w/Block Protect   This format is the same as parallel, except that the full block of side-by-side columns stays together, and the whole block moves to the next page if one column spills over.

5.   If you wish, you can customize the spacing between columns, the line spacing between rows in parallel columns, and the widths of individual columns. The sample page in the Columns dialog box will reflect each change you make.

6.   Choose OK.

WordPerfect inserts a [Col Def] code at the cursor position and turns the columns on.

To Define Columns
with the Power Bar and Ruler Bar

1. If they aren't visible, turn on the power bar (View ➤ Power Bar) and ruler bar (View ➤ Ruler Bar).

2. Use the Columns Define button in the power bar to define the number of columns you want.

3. If you want to adjust the column spacing, drag the column margin markers on the ruler bar to the desired position.

To Turn Columns On or Off

1. Position the cursor where you want to turn columns on or off. (The cursor must be to the right of the [Col Def] code that defines the columns.)

2. To turn columns off, choose Format ➤ Columns ➤ Off or click the Columns Define button in the power bar and choose Columns off. To turn columns on, choose Format ➤ Columns ➤ Define (or any other shortcut that opens the Columns dialog box), then choose OK.

To Edit Text in Columns

Use standard editing and cursor positioning techniques, with these exceptions:

- To *start a new column*, press Ctrl+⏎, or choose Format ➤ Columns ➤ Column Break, or click the Columns Define buton in the power bar and choose Column Break. Newspaper and balanced newspaper columns are started automatically, but you can start a new column earlier by inserting a column break. In parallel columns (or parallel columns with block protect), inserting a column break moves text to the next column.

- To *insert a page break*, press Ctrl+Shift+⏎, or choose Insert ➤ Page Break.

- To *move the cursor from column to column* without inserting text, use your mouse, or press Alt+← or Alt+→.

- To *move the cursor to the top or bottom* of the current column, press Alt+Home or Alt+End, respectively.

To Change the Number of Columns

Use either of the techniques below:

- To *change the number of columns,* position the cursor where you want the new number of columns to take effect. Then follow the steps above for defining columns and specify a different number of columns.

- To *delete the columnar format entirely*, turn on Reveal Codes (Alt+F3) and delete the column definition code [Col Def] and its associated page break codes [HPg] and [HCol-SP].

To Insert Column Separator Lines

1. Put the cursor in the columns where you want the column separators to begin.

2. Choose Format ➤ Columns ➤ Border/Fill.

3. From the Border Style drop-down list, choose Column Between.

4. Optionally, select (check) Apply Border To Current Column Group Only.

5. Choose OK.

NOTES You can set a columnar format before or after you've entered text and graphics. To prevent column separator lines from printing through graphics, print your document graphically. (See *Print*.)

You can't define columns within footnotes, endnotes, or tables.

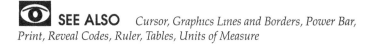

SEE ALSO *Cursor, Graphics Lines and Borders, Power Bar, Print, Reveal Codes, Ruler, Tables, Units of Measure*

COMBINE DOCUMENTS

You can combine WordPerfect documents by inserting another file anywhere within the current document.

To Insert a File into the Current Document

1. Position the cursor where you want to add the file.

2. Choose Insert ➤ File.

3. Type in the name of the desired file or highlight the name you want, then click Insert.

4. Choose Yes when asked "Insert file into current document?"

NOTES File ➤ Open opens a file in a new window.

SEE ALSO *File Management, Open*

COMMENT

You can use the Comment feature to add nonprinting comments to a document or to convert existing comments to text.

To Add a Comment to a Document

1. Move the cursor to where you want the comment to appear.

2. Choose Insert ➤ Comment ➤ Create. Or, right-click in the far left margin and choose Comment from the Quick-Menu. A comment editing window and feature bar will appear.

3. Type your comment as you would any text. You can also use the optional buttons in the Comment feature bar to in-sert your Initials or Name (see "To Customize Document Comments," below) and the system Date or Time.

4. If you want to edit the next or previous comment in the document, click the Next or Previous buttons in the Com-ment feature bar.

5. When you're done typing the comment, click the Close button in the Comment feature bar.

In Draft view, a shaded comment box will appear in your docu-ment and the comment text will be visible.

In Page or Two-Page view, a comment icon will appear in the left margin of the document window. You'll need to click the comment icon to see the comment text. (To hide the comment again, click anywhere in the document window).

To Change a Document Comment

Use any of the methods below to reach the comment editing window:

- Double-click the comment box or icon.

- Turn on Reveal Codes (Alt+F3) and double-click the [Com-ment] code.

- Move the cursor to just after the comment you want to change, then choose Insert ➤ Comment ➤ Edit.

- Right-click the comment icon or box and choose Edit.

Make whatever changes you wish, then click the Close button in
the Comment feature bar.

To Delete Comments

- To *delete one comment,* turn on Reveal Codes (Alt+F3) and
  delete the appropriate comment code [Comment]. Or,
  right-click the comment icon or box you want to delete,
  then choose Delete from the QuickMenu.

- To *delete all comments* in one step, press Ctrl+Home twice,
  then choose Edit ➤ Find and Relace (F2), choose Match ➤
  Codes, double-click *Comment* in the Find Codes list,
  choose Replace All, then choose Close.

To Convert Text to a Comment

1. Select the text that you want to convert to a comment.

2. Choose Insert ➤ Comment ➤ Create. Or, right-click in the
   far left margin and choose Comment from the QuickMenu.

To Convert a Comment to Text

1. Move the cursor just beyond the comment you want to
   convert to text.

2. Choose Insert ➤ Comment ➤ Convert To Text.

3. If necessary, add spaces or hard returns (⏎) to blend the
   newly converted text with existing text.

To Hide or Display Document Comments

1. Choose Edit ➤ Preferences and double-click Display.

2. To hide comments, clear the Comments check box. To display comments, check the Comments box.

3. Choose OK, then choose Close.

To Customize Document Comments

1. Choose Edit ➤ Preferences and double-click Environment.

2. In the User Info... area of the Environment Preferences dialog box, do any of the following:

- Choose Name, then type the name you want inserted when you click the Name button in the Comment feature bar.

- Choose Initials, then type the initials you want to appear in the comment icon and when you click the Initials button.

- Click the User Color button, then click the color you want to use as the background whenever you add a new comment.

3. Choose OK, then choose Close.

Your changes will affect new comments that you create (existing comments will be unaffected).

SEE ALSO *Delete, Document Window, Feature Bar, Reveal Codes, Selecting Text, View*

CONVERT CASE

This command converts selected text to UPPERCASE, lowercase, or Initial Cap Letters.

To Convert the Case of Selected Text

1. Select the text that you want to convert.

2. Choose Edit ➤ Convert Case.

3.   Choose either Lowercase, Uppercase, or Initial Capitals.

 **SEE ALSO**   *Selecting Text*

COUNTER

You can use Counters to count or number anything in your document, including paragraphs, chapters, sections, graphic boxes, widget names—whatever! WordPerfect has built-in system counters for the five types of graphic boxes. These counters are updated and displayed in captions automatically. However, you must manually increment, decrement, and display counters that you create.

To Create a Counter

1.   Position the cursor where you want to create a counter.

2.   Choose Insert ➤ Other ➤ Counter ➤ Create.

3.   In the Counter Name box, type a name for the counter.

4.   Specify the number of Levels (up to 5) and the Numbering Method for each level.

5.   Choose OK, then choose Close.

To Change or Display a Counter

1.   Position the cursor where you want the counter to change or to appear.

2.   Choose Insert ➤ Other ➤ Counter and highlight the counter and level you want to change or display.

3. Choose any of the following options as needed:

Edit Lets you change the highlighted counter's name, number of levels, and numbering method.

Delete Deletes the highlighted counter. You can only delete the counter itself, not an individual level. (Use Edit to reduce the number of levels in a counter.) You can't delete a built-in system counter.

Value Lets you set each level of the highlighted counter to a specific value.

Increase Increases the highlighted counter's value by 1.

Decrease Decreases the highlighted counter's value by 1.

Display In Document Displays the highlighted counter's value at the cursor position.

Increase and Display Increases the highlighted counter's value by 1 and displays it in your document.

Decrease and Display Decreases the highlighted counter's value by 1 and displays it in your document.

4. If necessary, choose Close.

👁 **SEE ALSO** *Cross-Reference, Graphics and Graphics Boxes, Line Numbering, Lists, Outline, Page Numbering*

CROSS-REFERENCE

You can use WordPerfect's automatic cross-referencing features to reference page numbers, paragraph or outline numbers, footnote and endnote numbers, and graphics box numbers.

References tell the reader to look somewhere else, as in "see Figure 5.3" or "see Footnote 4." A *target* is the place (such as a page number, figure, or table) where you're sending the reader.

Generating cross-references involves two processes:

- Set up the targets and references. You need to mark a target only once, then you can mark as many references to that target as you need. (You can define targets before references, or references before targets. However, the instructions below assume you're defining the targets first.)

- Generate the cross-references. (Choose Tools ➤ Generate, click the Generate button on the Cross-Reference feature bar, or press Ctrl+F9. Then choose OK.)

To Mark a Target

1. Choose Tools ➤ Cross-Reference to display the Cross-Reference feature bar.

2. Move the cursor just past the target. If necessary, use Reveal Codes (Alt+F3) to help you position the cursor. (When marking a page number target for a footnote or endnote, the cursor must be in the footnote or endnote.)

3. From the Reference drop-down list button in the feature bar, select the type of item you're targeting. Your options are Page, Secondary Page, Chapter, Volume, Paragraph/ Outline, Footnote, Endnote, Caption Number (for graphics boxes), and Counter (which will prompt for a counter name).

4. In the feature bar's Target text box, type a descriptive name for the target.

5. Click the Mark Target button in the feature bar.

To Mark a Reference

1. Choose Tools ➤ Cross-Reference to display the Cross-Reference feature bar.

2. Place the cursor where you want the reference to appear.

3.   Type any introductory text and then enter a blank space, if necessary. For example, type [**see page** and then press the spacebar.

4.   In the feature bar's Target text box, type the target name (exactly as you specified it when marking the target), or select the target name from the Target drop-down list.

5.   Click the Mark Reference button in the feature bar. (The question mark (?) in the reference will be replaced by the correct reference when you generate the lists and references.)

6.   Finish typing any introductory text for the reference. For instance, type a space and then] to finish the example started in step 3.

NOTES   You don't have to include text from the caption number style in your introductory text. WordPerfect will automatically insert text from the caption number style of any graphics box when it generates references. For instance, if you mark Figure 1 as a target, WordPerfect will insert the words Figure 1 in the reference automatically.

You must generate cross-references again if you make changes that affect the numbering of targets.

You can create cross-references for an individual document or for a master document (see the Master Document entry).

To delete a cross reference or target, turn on Reveal Codes (Alt+F3) and delete the appropriate [Ref] or [Target] code.

You can combine cross-references, as in the examples below:

- References to multiple targets of different types (e.g., *see page 1, Figure 2*). For this example, you'd define a Page target and Caption Number target, then create the references to each target as described above.

- References to multiple targets with the same reference type (e.g., *see pages 10, 12, 14*). For this example, you'd define three Page targets. Then create the references to each target as described above.

- Page *x* of *y* references in headers and footers. For this example, create a Page target on the last page (name it **Last Page**). Then create a header or footer, type **Page** and a space, and use the Number button in the Header/Footer feature bar to insert the page number. Type **of** and a space, then insert a reference to the **Last Page** target. For a quicker method, run the PAGEXOFY macro that comes with WordPerfect. (See *Macros*.)

👁 **SEE ALSO**   *Counter; Footnotes and Endnotes; Generate; Graphics and Graphics Boxes; Headers, Footers, and Watermarks; Lists; Macros; Master Document; Outline; Page Numbering; Tables*

CURSOR

The *cursor* (or *insertion point*) shows where the next character that you type will appear in the document window or in Reveal Codes. On the document window, the cursor is usually a small, blinking vertical bar. In Reveal Codes, the cursor is a solid block. You can position the cursor with the mouse or the keyboard (whichever is easiest for you).

To Move the Cursor with the Mouse

- Position the mouse pointer just before the character (or code) and click the left mouse button. (If the character or code isn't visible, use the scroll bar to bring it into view.)

The mouse pointer usually appears as an I-beam on the document window. In Reveal Codes, it appears as an I-beam when pointing to text and as an arrow when pointing to a code.

To Move the Cursor with the Keyboard

- Press a cursor movement key or key combination (e.g., arrow keys, Home, End, Ctrl+→, Ctrl+←). For most operations, you can press the positioning keys shown in Table I.

Table I: Keyboard Methods for Moving the Cursor
(Most Operations)

TO MOVE TO	PRESS
Beginning of document (after any codes)	Ctrl+Home
Beginning of document (before any codes)	Ctrl+Home twice
Beginning of line (after any codes)	Home
Beginning of line (before any codes)	Home twice
Bottom of screen (then down one screen at a time)	PgDn
Down one line	↓
Down one paragraph	Ctrl+↓
End of document (after any codes)	Ctrl+End
End of line (after any codes)	End
First line on previous page	Alt+PgUp
First line on next page	Alt+PgDn
Left one character	←
Left one word	Ctrl+←
Right one character	→
Right one word	Ctrl+→
Top of screen (then up one screen at a time)	PgUp
Up one line	↑
Up one paragraph	Ctrl+↑

NOTES   You must position the cursor before adding, changing, deleting, or moving text and most formatting codes. You can either type over or insert characters at the cursor.

You can't move the cursor beyond the last character or code in a document or before the first code.

If the cursor doesn't seem to move when you're at the document window, it may be resting on a hidden code. Continue moving the cursor past the code, or turn on Reveal Codes (Alt+F3) to make the code visible.

To customize the behavior of the cursor when it moves through hidden codes, choose Edit ➤ Preferences and double-click Environment. Then select or deselect Confirm Deletion Of Codes, Stop Insertion Point At Hidden Codes. Choose OK and Close.

SEE ALSO   *Codes, Document Window, Go To, Insert/Type-over, Mouse, Reveal Codes*

CUT, COPY, AND PASTE

Use cut, copy, and paste to move or copy selected data within and between documents, including those in other Windows applications. Copying leaves the original data intact. Cutting removes it from the original position.

To Cut, Copy, and Paste Data

1.   Select the data you want to cut or copy.

2.   Choose Edit ➤ Cut (Ctrl+X or Shift+Del), or Edit ➤ Copy (Ctrl+C or Ctrl+Ins). Or right-click the selected data and choose Cut or Copy from the QuickMenu. (If the Clipboard already contains some data, you can add the selected data to the end of the Clipboard by choosing Edit ➤ Append.)

3. Move the cursor to where you want the data to appear. If it's another WordPerfect document, open that document and position the cursor. If it's another application, open the application and file and position the cursor.

4. Use any of the following methods to paste the data at the cursor position:

- In a WordPerfect document, choose Edit ➤ Paste (Ctrl+V or Shift+Ins), or right-click and select Paste from the QuickMenu. The pasted text will have its original formatting attributes (for example, boldface or underlining). If you'd rather the pasted text have the same formatting attributes as the text at the cursor position, press Ctrl+Shift+V (Paste Simple) instead.

- In another application, you can choose Edit ➤ Paste (Ctrl+V or Shift+Ins). Or, if the application supports object linking and embedding, you can choose Edit ➤ Paste Link or Edit ➤ Paste Special. (See the Object Linking and Embedding Entry and your application's documentation for details.)

NOTES The Windows Clipboard maintains its data until you cut or copy more data or exit Windows. You can paste from the Clipboard to as many locations as you want.

The toolbar provides handy shortcuts for Cut, Copy, and Paste.

To view what's on the Clipboard, you can run the CLIPBRD macro that comes with WordPerfect. Or, see your Windows documentation for other methods.

SEE ALSO *Append, Drag and Drop, Marcos, Object Linking and Embedding, Selecting Text, Undo/Redo*

DATE/TIME

The Date/Time command allows you to insert the current date and/or time as either code or text.

To Set the Date/Time Format

1. Choose Insert ➤ Date ➤ Date Format.

2. Highlight a format from the list of Predefined Formats, and optionally customize that format using the Custom button.

3. Choose OK to return.

These settings affect only dates that you add to the current document beyond the current cursor position.

To Insert the Date/ Time in a Document

1. Move the cursor to where you want the date to appear, then choose Insert ➤ Date.

2. Choose either Date Text or Date Code, depending on which you want to insert.

Alternatively, you can double-click the date in the status bar, or press Ctrl+D to insert date text, or Ctrl+Shift+D to insert the date code.

NOTES If you enter a code, it will automatically be updated to reflect the current system date whenever you retrieve or print the document. Dates entered as text will *not* be updated. The system date and time are determined by the DOS commands DATE and TIME, and the Date/Time applet in the Windows Control Panel.

 **SEE ALSO** *Initial Codes Style, Merge Operations*

DECIMAL ALIGNMENT

The decimal align character (initially ".") is used to vertically align tabbed text or text in tables, and the thousands separator (initially ",") is used to align numbers in math calculations.

To Change the Alignment Character

1. Move the cursor to above the first number you want to realign.

2. Choose Format ➤ Line ➤ Tab Set.

3. In the Character text box under Align Character, delete the existing character and type the character that you want the numbers to align on, or press Ctrl+W and select a character from the WordPerfect Characters dialog box. Then choose OK.

Only decimal-aligned text that's below the cursor position and contains the character you specified in step 3 will be aligned on that character.

To Change the Thousands Separator

1. Move the cursor to above the first number you want to realign.

2. Choose Format ➤ Line ➤ Other Codes ➤ Thousands Separator.

3. In the Thousands Separator text box, type the character that you want to use as a thousands separator, or press Ctrl+W and select a character from the WordPerfect Characters dialog box.

4. Choose Insert.

 **SEE ALSO** *Tables, Tabs*

DELAY CODES

This feature lets you insert page formatting codes that won't take effect until a certain page. For example, you can define page formatting codes for headers, footers, or page numbers at the top of a document, but delay the execution of those codes until a certain page (i.e., after the title page, Table of Contents, and so forth).

To Delay Formatting Codes

1. Move the cursor to the top of the document, or to any location before the page where you want formatting to take effect.

2. Choose Format ➤ Page ➤ Delay Codes.

3. Specify the number of pages (from the current page) to delay the new codes, and choose OK.

4. A Define Delayed Codes editing window and feature bar will appear. Create the features you want to delay just as you normally would when editing a document. Or, use the feature bar buttons to specify a Paper Size or create an Image, Header/Footer, or Watermark. Each time you finish setting up a feature, WordPerfect will add that feature's code to the Define Delayed Codes editing window.

5. When you're done entering codes to delay, choose the Close button in the feature bar.

To Change a Delay Code

To edit a Delay code(s) feature, double-click the [Delay] code you want to change and make modifications as necessary. When you are done, choose the Close button on the feature bar.

NOTES   Only open codes and graphics can be delayed. Paired codes and some codes used in formatting such as Indent, Center, Flush Right, and Tab cannot be delayed.

 **SEE ALSO** *Graphics and Graphics Boxes; Headers, Footers, and Watermarks; Initial Codes Style; Page Numbering; Paper Size*

DELETE

Use this command to delete anything in your document. If you make a mistake, you can instantly undelete it.

To Delete Text and Codes

Use any method below:

- Press Delete (Del) to delete the character (or code) to the right of the cursor.

- Press Backspace to delete the character (or code) to the left of the cursor.

- Select the text (or codes) you want to delete, then press Delete (Del) or Backspace.

- Use one of the following shortcut keys:

Key	What It Does
Ctrl+Backspace	Delete word
Ctrl+Del	Delete to end of line
Ctrl+Shift+Del	Delete to end of page

To Delete a Code from Reveal Codes

- Move the mouse pointer to the code you want to delete, then drag the code off of the Reveal Codes screen (up into the document window).

To Delete a Table

1. Move the mouse pointer to one of the lines inside the table, until it becomes a vertical or horizontal arrow (not the usual angled arrow).

2. Triple-click the mouse button to select all the cells in the table.

3. Press Delete (Del), choose Entire Table, then choose OK.

To Delete a Graphics Box

- Click the graphics box once to select it, then press Delete (Del).

- Or drag the hidden code for the graphics box off of the Reveal Codes screen.

To Undelete

1. Move the cursor back to the place where you made the ac-cidental deletion, or to wherever you want the material to reappear.

2. Choose Edit ➤ Undelete, or press Ctrl+Shift+Z.

3. Choose Restore. (See Undelete for more information.)

To Delete a File

1. First, make sure that the file you want to delete isn't open in any applications. (Close the file if it's open in WordPerfect.)

2. Choose File ➤ Open (Ctrl+O).

3. Highlight the name of the file you want to delete, then choose File Options ➤ Delete or press Del.

4. Choose Delete again at the prompt.

5. Choose Cancel in the Open File dialog box to return to your document.

You cannot use WordPerfect's Undelete to undelete a file. Instead, you'll need to use the DOS UNDELETE command, File ➤ Undelete in the Windows File Manager (if available), or a third-party utility program.

 NOTES   To delete a code or item of text throughout the document, use the Edit ➤ Find And Replace (F2) commands to re-place the text/codes you want to delete with "nothing."

Deleting one code of a paired code (e.g., [Bold] or [Italc]) automat-ically deletes the other code.

SEE ALSO   *Replace, Selecting Text, Undelete, Undo/Redo*

DIALOG BOXES

A dialog box appears whenever you choose a menu option that requires additional information.

To Make Selections in a Dialog Box

The current default option within a dialog box is outlined with a dashed line or is highlighted. You can use any of the following meth-ods to choose an option:

- Click on the option you want.

- Press Tab (to move forward) or Shift+Tab (to move back-ward) to highlight or outline the item you want. Then click the option or press the spacebar to select it.

- If the option you want has an underlined letter, you can choose the option by holding down Alt and typing that let-ter. (If necessary, click the option or press alt+↓, or press the spacebar to open the options menu or list box.)

- If the option is a toggle (like a check box), use the spacebar, or click, to turn it on and off.

To Save/Abandon Dialog Box Selections

If you want to save and activate your selections in a dialog box, choose Close or OK. If you want to abandon the current dialog box without saving any selections, choose the Cancel button or press Esc.

NOTES   All Windows applications use dialog boxes with similar controls. To learn more about dialog boxes, please refer to your Windows documentation.

SEE ALSO   *Menus, Windows*

DOCUMENT COMPARE

This feature compares the document on the screen to another document on disk (presumably an earlier version of the same document). WordPerfect marks phrases in the current document that differ from the stored version.

To Compare Two Documents

1.   Open one of the documents that you want to compare and choose File ➤ Compare Document ➤ Add Markings.

2.   Enter the name, and, if necessary, the path of the document on disk that you want to compare to your current document. Or, click the file button and select a different path and file name.

3.   Choose the Word, Phrase, Sentence, or Paragraph option, depending on how you want to compare the two documents.

4.   Choose OK.

Redline and strikeout codes are inserted to surround the changed phrases. Deleted phrases appear with a line drawn through the text. Added phrases appear in red if you have a color monitor.

To Remove Marks from a Document

- Choose File ➤ Compare Document ➤ Remove Markings, select Remove Redline Markings And Strikeout Text or Remove Strikeout Text Only, and click OK.

- Or, choose Edit ➤ Undo (Ctrl+Z) immediately after you compare the documents.

SEE ALSO   *Font*

DOCUMENT INFO

Document Info displays statistics about the current document.

To Display Document Statistics

1.   Choose File ➤ Document Info.

2.   After reviewing the results, choose OK.

NOTES   The grammar checker (Grammatik) also provides statistics about your document.

SEE ALSO   *Grammatik*

DOCUMENTS/BACKUP

Documents/Backup can automatically back up files in two ways: by saving documents at timed intervals and by saving a copy of the original file each time you replace it with a newer version.

To Control Timed and Original Backups

1. Select Edit ➤ Preferences and double-click File.

2. Select from the the following options:

Default Directory Accept the default directory, or change as needed.

Use Default Extension On Open And Save Accept default extension (WPD), or change as needed.

Backup Directory Specify the directory where you want timed backups to appear. If you leave this option blank, timed backups will be stored in the same directory as your WIN.COM program (usually c:\windows).

Timed Document Backup Every *n* Minutes Make timed backups. You must enter the number of minutes between saves; 10 minutes is the default.

Original Document Backup Back up the original file.

3. Choose OK, then choose Close.

NOTES If the timed backup files exist the next time you start WordPerfect, you'll be asked to rename, open, or delete them before being taken to the document window. If you open them, you can recover all your work up to the moment of interruption. If you delete them, they are lost forever. Timed backups are named WP{WP}.BK*n*, where *n* is the document number of the backup file.

Original backups are always stored in the same directory as your document file. The old version of the file is named *filename.BK!* and will remain on disk after you exit WordPerfect.

When you recover an original backup file, rename it immediately with File ➤ Save As to remove the .BK! extension.

 **SEE ALSO** *Preferences, Save/Save As*

DOCUMENT SUMMARY

Document summary allows you to create summary information about a document. Use this information to help you locate and identify documents in the future.

To Create or Edit a Summary

1. Choose File ➤ Document Summary.

2. Fill in any descriptive text you want. Optionally, you can use the Configure button to choose other fields to display in the summary. You can also choose the Options button to print, delete, extract or save the summary information.

3. Choose OK.

 **SEE ALSO** *Print*

DOCUMENT WINDOW

The document window is where most editing operations take place. The *cursor (*also called the *insertion point)* indicates where the next character that you type will appear.

To Open a Document Window

• To start a new document in an empty document window, press Ctrl+N or Shift+F4, or click the New Blank Document button in the WordPerfect toolbar.

- To start and fill in a new document with predefined text, you can use a *template*. Choose File ➤ New, press Ctrl+T, or click the New Document button in the WordPerfect toolbar. Then click an appropriate group in the Group list of the New Document dialog box, and double-click the template you want in the Select Template list. Respond to any prompts that appear.

- To open an existing document in its own window, choose File ➤ Open (Ctrl+O).

NOTES   You can have up to nine document windows on-screen at a time, but only one can be active. The active document window will be in the foreground with its title bar colored differently. To switch from one window to another, click on the title bar or choose the document window name from the Window menu. Or, press Ctrl+F6 to switch to the next document and Ctrl+Shift+F6 to switch to the previous document.

Use the standard Windows techniques to maximize, minimize, size, and move the document window (see your Windows manual if you need help). Choose Window ➤ Cascade Horizontal, or Window ➤ Tile or Window ➤ Tile Vertical to rearrange the document windows on your screen.

Shift+F4 opens a new, cascaded document window on the screen.

SEE ALSO   *File Management, New, Open, Reveal Codes, Template*

DRAG AND DROP

This command lets you move and copy text using the mouse instead of menus or shortcut keys.

To Drag and Drop Text

1. Select the text you want to move or copy.

2. Move the pointer to the selected text and hold down the mouse button. A small icon appears on the pointer.

3. If you want to copy rather than move the text, hold down the Ctrl key.

4. Drag the mouse pointer to the new location for the text. You can scroll off any edge of the screen to keep moving in that direction.

5. When the mouse pointer gets to the destination for the moved or copied text, release the mouse button. If you copied text, release the Ctrl key *after* releasing the mouse button.

 **NOTES** You can drag and drop to another place in the current document window, to another WordPerfect document window, or to another application that supports OLE 2. The last two drag-and-drop locations are new in version 6.1.

 **SEE ALSO** *Cut, Copy, and Paste; Object Linking and Embedding; Selecting Text*

DRAW

You can use Draw to create a new drawing or to modify an existing image. Draw was improved significantly for WordPerfect version 6.1.

To Start Draw

- To create a new drawing from scratch, choose <u>G</u>raphics ➤ <u>D</u>raw or click the Draw button on the WordPerfect toolbar.

- To in-place edit an existing image without leaving the WordPerfect document window, double-click the image. Or, right-click the image and choose Drawing Object ➤ Edit. You can also select the graphics box that contains the image and choose Edit ➤ Drawing Object ➤ Edit.

- To edit an existing image in a separate WP Draw window, right-click the image and choose Drawing Object ➤ Open, or select the graphics box that contains the image and choose Edit ➤ Drawing Object ➤ Open.

Once you get into WP Draw, use the tools in the toolbox (Figure 2 on the next page) or equivalent commands in the Insert and Format menus to create a new drawing or embellish an existing one. If you are editing a separate WP Draw window, you'll find instructions at the bottom of the screen after selecting a tool.

A summary of all the tool available on the pull-down menus appears below:

File   When in-place editing, contains general commands for managing the *WordPerfect document.* When editing in a separate WP Draw window, contains commands for returning to WordPerfect and for saving the drawing to disk.

Edit   Lets you undo, delete, cut, copy, paste, select, edit, and rotate a selected object, and choose preferences.

View   Lets you hide/display the toolbar, ruler, and grid and lets you zoom in and out on the drawing. Also lets you customize the grid snap.

Insert   Includes options for selecting drawing tools, creating charts and images, adding text, using scanned images, and inserting files and objects.

Format   Lets you change the font, color, fill, line, and other attributes of the currently selected item, as well as for items you're about to draw.

Graphics   Lets you move selected items to the front or back; flip, group, or separate items; and contour text.

Tools   Lets you use WordPerfect's writing tools and run macros.

Window   Provides standard commands for arranging and choosing windows.

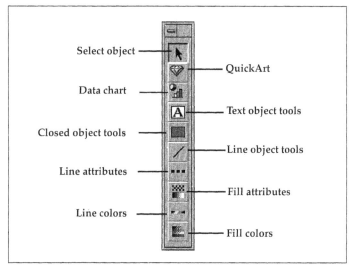

Figure 2: The WordPerfect Draw Toolbox

Help Offers standard Help options. To get help with drawing, choose Help ➤ How Do I, then click *Draw And Edit Objects* and select topics as needed.

To Save a Drawing

When you're finished creating or modifying a drawing, use any method below:

- Click the Close button in the toolbar. (This saves the drawing, returns you to WordPerfect, and deselects the graphics box.)

- If you are editing in-place, click in the document window, outside the drawing box. (This saves the drawing, returns you to WordPerfect, and selects the box.)

- If you are editing in a separate WP Draw application window and *do not want* to save your changes, choose File ➤ Close And Return To Document.

- If you are editing in a separate WP Draw application window and *do want* to save your changes, choose File ➤ Exit And Return To Document.

NOTES If you're not an artist and you use pre-drawn clip art often, you might prefer the much simpler Image Tools, discussed under Graphics Editor.

Though readily accessible from WordPerfect for Windows, WP Draw is actually a separate application. For more information on Draw, please refer to the WordPerfect Draw Booklet that came with your WordPerfect program.

SEE ALSO *Chart, Graphics and Graphics Boxes, Graphics Editor, TextArt*

Drop caps add instant drama to your documents by enlarging one or more characters (or the word) at the start of a paragraph. Use drop caps to spice up chapter openings, newsletters, brochures, advertisements, and more.

To Create a Drop Cap

1. Put the cursor where you are about to type a new paragraph, or anywhere in an existing paragraph.

2. Choose Format ➤ Drop Cap, or press Ctrl+Shift+C. The Drop cap feature bar will appear, along with a drop cap at the start of the paragraph (assuming the paragraph isn't empty).

3. If necessary, type the paragraph.

4. If necessary, change the drop cap appearance as explained in the following section.

5. When you're finished, click the Close button in the feature bar.

To Change the Drop Cap Appearance

1. Put the cursor in the paragraph whose drop cap you want to change. (This can even be a paragraph that doesn't have a drop cap yet.)

2. If the Drop Cap feature bar is not visible, choose Format ➤ Drop Cap or press Ctrl+Shift+C.

3. Choose buttons in the Drop Cap feature bar, as described below:

- To *select another style of drop cap,* click Type, then click the sample for the style you want.

- To *change the drop cap's size* (in number of lines), click Size, then choose a size.

- To *change the drop cap's position,* click Position, then choose a position.

- To *change the drop cap's font,* click Font, choose appropriate font options, and choose OK.

- To *add a border or fill,* click Border/Fill, choose appropriate border options and fill options, and choose OK.

- To *change the number of characters in the drop cap* and control other appearance options, click Options. Choose the options you want, then choose OK.

4. When you're finished, click the Close button in the Drop Cap feature bar.

To Remove a Drop Cap

1. Put the cursor in the paragraph whose drop cap you want to remove, then choose Format ➤ Drop Cap (Ctrl+Shift+C).

2. Click the Type button in the Drop Cap feature bar, then click NO CAP (the last entry in the list of sample styles).

3. Click the Close button in the feature bar.

NOTES   This feature inserts a [Dropcap Definition] code at the start of the paragraph. To open the Drop Cap feature bar quickly, double-click the [Dropcap Definition] code in Reveal Codes.

You can also use TextArt to create fancy text characters and position them anywhere in the document.

SEE ALSO   *Font, Graphics Lines and Borders, TextArt*

ENVELOPE

Use the Envelope feature to type an envelope easily.

To Type an Envelope

1. If available, select the text for the mailing address and then choose Format ➤ Envelope.

2. Optionally, fill in the Return Addresses portion of the Envelope dialog box and select (check) Print Return Address. If you've previously created envelopes in WordPerfect, you can choose to:

- Accept the current return address.
- Select an address from the drop-down list.
- Select <New Address> from the drop-down list and type in a new address.
- Add the current address to the drop-down list by choosing the Add button.

- Delete an address from the drop-down list by highlighting that address in the drop-down list, choosing the Delete button, and choosing Yes.

- Change the font for the address by choosing the Font button and selecting a font (see the Font entry).

- Hide the return address by deselecting (unchecking) the Print Return Address option if it is already selected.

3. Fill in the Mailing Addresses box if you didn't select text for the mailing address in step 1. The procedure is basically the same as for filling in a return address, except that you choose options in the right side of the dialog box.

4. If you wish, choose any of the options below:

- To *change the envelope size,* select a size from the Envelope Definitions drop-down list.

- To *create a new envelope size,* choose Create New Definition, specify the paper size options for an envelope including a Paper Name, and choose OK.

- To *print a POSTNET Bar Code* above or below the mailing address, choose Options, select one of the Include And Position options in the USPS Bar Code Options area of the Envelope Options dialog box and choose OK. WordPerfect will retrieve the POSTNET Bar Code from the mailing address automatically . If the bar code does not appear, click on the POSTNET Bar code text box, and (if necessary) enter or edit the postal code.

- To *change the position of the return or mailing addresses* on the envelope, choose Options, adjust the horizontal and vertical position of the appropriate address, and choose OK. WordPerfect will use the selected positions whenever you use the current envelope definition.

5. If you want to print your envelope immediately, choose Print Envelope. If you want to save the envelope information in the current document (without printing), choose Append To Doc.

If you chose to print your envelope in step 5, insert the envelope into the printer according to your printer manual's instructions.

 **SEE ALSO** *Bar Code, Paper Size*

EQUATIONS

The Equation Editor lets you create, edit, and align mathematical and scientific equations.

To Create an Equation

1. Move the cursor where you want the equation to appear in the document and choose Graphics ➤ Equation. You'll be taken to the Equation Editor.

2. Type the equation in the top half of the window, or use the Commands pop-up list to choose an Equation Palette, then double-click on the element you want to select in the Equation Palette.

3. To check your progress, choose View ➤ Redisplay (Ctrl+F3) or click the Redisplay button in the toolbar.

4. When you've finished, choose File ➤ Close (Ctrl+F4) or click the Close button in the toolbar.

To Edit an Equation

• Double-click the equation you want to change in the document window to get back to the Equation Editor.

To Delete an Equation

• Drag the Box code out of the Reveal Codes window or click the equation once, then press Delete (Del).

NOTES To control how elements of the equation are arranged, enclose portions of the equation in curly braces, as in the example below.

Equation Typed As...	Is Displayed As...
A+B OVER X+Y	$A + \dfrac{B}{X} + Y$
{A+B} OVER {X+Y}	$\dfrac{A+B}{X+Y}$

The Equation Editor lets you edit and select font options for equations with all the special symbols and typesetting standards. However, it does not solve the equations for you.

SEE ALSO *Characters, Graphics and Graphics Boxes*

EXIT

The Exit command closes WordPerfect and returns you to the Program Manager. You should always save your work and exit WordPerfect prior to turning off your computer.

To Exit WordPerfect

1. Choose File ➤ Exit, press Alt+F4, or double-click WordPerfect's Control-menu box.

2. If you have made changes to any open document, the prompt "Save changes to <filename>?" appears. Choose Yes to save, No to exit without saving the current file, or Cancel to abandon the operation and stay in WordPerfect.

3. If you chose Yes in step 2 and the file has yet to be saved, the Save As dialog box will appear. Enter a file name and choose OK.

To Exit the Current Document

- Choose File ➤ Close (Ctrl+F4) or double-click the document's Control-menu box.

If you have made changes to the document since the last time you saved it and do not want those changes to take effect, then answer No to the "Save changes to Document?" prompt.

 **NOTES**   If you have multiple documents open when you exit WordPerfect, you will be prompted to save each document that has been modified since last saved.

SEE ALSO   *Save/Save As*

FEATURE BAR

Feature bars provide shortcuts for specific WordPerfect features and pop up only when they're needed. For example, when you choose Insert ➤ Comment ➤ Create, you'll see the Comment feature bar shown below.

The following feature bars appear when you choose the related menu options or shortcuts: Table Formula, Outline, Index, Table Of

Contents, List, Cross-Reference, Table Of Authorities, Hypertext, Drop Cap, Graphics Box, Header/Footer, Footnote/Endnote, Watermark, Merge, Template, Comment, Sound, ToA Full Form, Delay Codes, Caption, Text Box, Macro Edit, Template Macro Edit.

To Use a Feature Bar

- Click the button you want, or hold down the Alt and Shift keys while you press the underlined letter in the button name. For example, you can select the Close button by clicking it, or by pressing Alt+Shift+C.

NOTES You can't customize the appearance of feature bars, nor can you move them.

To find out what a button on the feature bar does, move the mouse pointer to the button and look at the WordPerfect title bar.

The following buttons generally appear in every feature bar:

? Click this button if you want to select a different feature bar or if you want to choose options from a menu instead of clicking buttons on the feature bar. Right-click this button (or the feature bar) to select a different feature bar or to get help.

Close Choose this button when you're done using the feature bar and want to clear it from the screen. In some cases, choosing Close also will close whatever editing window you're using. (If you're using the Macro Edit or Template Macro Edit feature bar choose Options, then Close Macro or Remove Macro Bar.)

⦿ **SEE ALSO** *Power Bar, Toolbar*

FILE MANAGEMENT

WordPerfect 6.1 for Windows does not have its own dedicated built-in file manager. However, you can manage files through the Open File and Save As dialog boxes. The dialog box in Figure 3 is typical of what you might see when opening or saving a file.

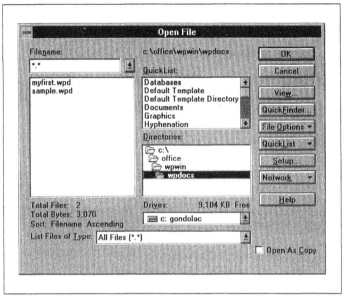

Figure 3: The Open File dialog box

To Manage Files

1. Go to a dialog box that opens or saves a file. For example, choose File ➤ Open (Ctrl+O).

2. If necessary, choose a drive from the Drives drop-down list, and a directory from the Directories or QuickList areas.

3. Select the name of the file(s) you want to copy, move, delete, or whatever (see below).

4. Choose File Options, and then select whichever option is appropriate to what you want to do (i.e., Copy, Move, Rename, Delete, and so forth). Or, right-click the file list, QuickList, or Directories list and choose a QuickMenu option. See Options, below.

5. Respond to any prompts or instructions on the screen. Choose OK or Cancel to close the dialog box when you're done.

To Search for a Document

If the file you're looking for is on another *drive* and/or *directory*, you can search for it:

1. Go to a dialog box that opens or saves a file. For example, choose <u>F</u>ile ➤ <u>O</u>pen (Ctrl+O) in the file list below the File-name (or Directory <u>N</u>ame) text box.

2. To list a different group of file names, use any of the methods below:

- If the file is on a different drive, choose the drive you want from the Dri<u>v</u>es drop-down list.

- If the file is on a different directory, choose the directory you want from the <u>D</u>irectories list. (For example, double-click the directory you want or highlight it and press ↵.)

- To list files of a different type, click the List Files of <u>T</u>ype (or Save Files As <u>T</u>ype) drop-down list and select a file type. Choose the top entry in the list if you want to display all files (*.*).

- To specify the drive, directory, and file type all at once, type the full path name and wildcards into the text box above the list of files and press ↵. For example, typing **c:\mydocs\e*.*** into the box would list all files in the \MYDOCS directory on drive C that start with **e**.

3. When the list shows the file name you want to work with, you can do any of the following:

- Click on or use the arrow keys to highlight the file name in the file list. The highlighted file name will appear in the text box above the file list. Then click OK in the dialog box.

- Double-click the file name you want. This completes the operation you chose in step 1 (for example, to open the file).

To Select More than One File

Use standard Windows techniques (summarized below) to select multiple files in the file list. After selecting the files, choose OK (to open up to nine files) or use the File Options button to manage the files. (See *Options,* below.)

- To *select several adjacent file names,* click the first file name (or highlight it and press the spacebar). Then hold down Shift, and click the last file or press ↓ until you highlight the last file. To select all files, click in the file list and press Ctrl+/.

- To *select several non-adjacent file names* with the mouse, click on the first file name, then hold down Ctrl while clicking each additional file name.

- To *deselect multiple selected files,* click on any file name or press the spacebar.

- To *deselect one file without deselecting others,* hold down Ctrl and click on the file name you want to deselect. Or, press Shift+F8, use the ↑ or ↓ key to select the file name you want to deselect, and press the spacebar. When you are finished, press Shift+F8 again.

To Use the File Button

Many text boxes that allow you to enter a file or directory name have a file button at one end. If you're not sure of the file or directory name (or don't wish to type it), click the file button or move the cursor to the text box and press Alt+↓ or F4. A Select File or Select Directory dialog box will open. Use the techniques described above to locate the name you want, then double-click the name or highlight it and choose OK to return to the original dialog box.

OPTIONS   Most or all of these buttons are available in dialog boxes that open or save files:

View   Opens the Viewer window, which lets you look at most files without opening them first. To see what's in a file, select it and click the View button, and it will appear in the Viewer window. Maximize, restore, resize, or close the Viewer window as needed. To search through the file shown, click on the Viewer window and press F2 to open the Find dialog box. (See the Find entry for more information.) Right-click the Viewer Window to display a QuickMenu of options.

QuickFinder Lets you use QuickFinder to locate files that contain certain text. (See the QuickFinder entry for more information.)

File Options Lets you choose from these file management commands: Copy (copies one or more files), Move (moves one or more files to a new location), Rename (renames a file), Delete (deletes one or more files), Change Attributes (changes file attributes of one or more files), Print (prints one or more WordPerfect files), Print File List (prints a list of selected file names or the entire list of file names), Create Directory (creates a new directory), Remove Directory (deletes the highlighted directory list, or whichever directory you specify), Rename Directory (renames the highlighted directory, or whichever directory you specify). Instead of choosing File Options ➤ Delete, you can press the Del key.

QuickList Lets you choose whether the directory list includes the directory list, QuickList, or both; and lets you edit the QuickList. (See the QuickList entry for more information.)

Help Provides help on file management operations.

NOTES You can also use the Windows File Manager to manage files. Press Alt+Tab until you get to the Program Manager, then open the Main group and open File Manager. See your Windows documentation for more information.

SEE ALSO *Combine Documents, Find, New, Open, QuickFinder, QuickList, Save/Save As*

FIND

This command lets you locate a particular character, phrase, word form, or code in your document.

To Use Find

1. Move the cant to begin the searchursor to where you w or select a chunk of text to search, then choose Edit ➤ Find or press F2.

2. Make sure the cursor is in the Find and Replace text box, then:

- To *search for a particular word or phrase*, type the text you're looking for.

- To *include a special character* in the search, press Ctrl+W and add the character as you normally would when typing a document.

- To *search for a general code*, choose Match ➤ Codes and select the code you want to look for. Then choose Insert in the Codes dialog box.

- To *search for a specific code*, choose Type ➤ Specific Codes, select the code you want to search for, then click OK in the Specific Codes dialog box.

- To *make the search more specific*, **choose** Match, then choose Whole Word, Case, and/or Font as appropriate.

- To *search for various forms of a word*, select (check) Type ➤ Word Forms, then type a single word into the Find text box. For example, if you select Word Forms and then type **drive** into the Find text box, WordPerfect will match words such as **drive, drove, driven, driving,** and so on. (This is new in version 6.1.)

3. Optionally, open the Direction menu in the dialog box and choose a direction for the search (either Forward or Backward).

4. Optionally, open the Actio_n_ menu in the dialog box and choose an action to take when a match occurs. Your choices are _S_elect Match (the default), Position _B_efore, Po-sition _A_fter, and _E_xtend Selection.

5. Optionally, open the _O_ptions menu and choose where the search should begin. Your choices are _B_egin Find At Top Of Document, _W_rap At Beg./End Of Document, _L_imit Find Within Selection (if you selected text in step 1), and _I_nclude Headers, Footers, etc. In Find.

6. To begin the search, choose _F_ind Next. Repeat this step as needed. (You can click in the document window if neces-sary, and then click the dialog box again to continue searching.)

7. When you're done searching, choose _C_lose to close the Find And Replace Text dialog box.

To repeat the previous search after you've closed the Find And Re-place Text dialog box, press Shift+F2 to search forward or Alt+F2 to search backward.

NOTES In version 6.1, the Find and Replace options on the _E_dit menu were combined into a single option (_E_dit ➤ _F_ind And Replace). See _Replace_ for details on replacing text and/or codes.

SEE ALSO _Font, Go To, Replace, Selecting Text_

FONT

Use the Font command to change the typeface, size, and appear-ance of any text in your document.

To Select a Font or Attribute

1. Move the cursor where you want to make the change. Or, if you want to change the font/attribute of existing text, select that text.

2. Choose Format ➤ Font (F9), then choose a Font Face, Font Style, Font Size, Appearance, Position, Relative Size, and Color Options as needed from the Font dialog box.

3. Choose OK to return to your document.

If you selected text in step 1, only that text will be displayed with the new attribute or font in the new font. If you didn't select text, all text beyond the cursor will appear in the new font until another font code is inserted in the document.

As a shortcut, repeat step 1 above. Then use the Font Face and Font Size buttons in the power bar to select the typeface and size you want.

NOTES   WordPerfect cannot create fonts. It can only use fonts that are built into your printer and fonts that you've purchased and installed separately. Typically, you use Windows (rather than WordPerfect) to install optional third-party fonts.

SEE ALSO   *Font Setup, Make It Fit Expert, Power Bar, Selecting Text*

FONT SETUP

To display and print fonts in WordPerfect, those fonts must already be set up. WordPerfect can take advantage of today's modern graphics fonts such as TrueType (which is built into Windows) or Type 1 (through the Adobe Type Manager, abbreviated as ATMl). You can also use older printer fonts from cartridges and download-able soft fonts (though these old style fonts are falling into disuse because they are inconvenient).

To Install Graphics Fonts

To install graphics fonts, follow the font manufacturer's instructions. The fonts will be installed in your Windows printer drivers, and Word-Perfect can use them whenever you chose the appropriate printer.

If you're installing TrueType fonts and need help, refer to your Windows documentation. You may need to use the Font applet in the Windows Control Panel to install and activate the fonts.

To Install Printer Fonts

To install non-graphics fonts such as cartridges and downloadable soft fonts, follow the font manufacturer's instructions. You can also search for the topic *Downloading and Installing Soft Fonts* in the WordPerfect's online Help.

👁 **SEE ALSO** *Font, Print*

FOOTNOTES AND ENDNOTES

Use footnotes or endnotes to list sources or to provide more de-tailed information about an item in your text. Footnotes print at the bottom of the page where they are referenced. Endnotes are usually placed at the end of the document. Because footnote and endnote commands work almost identically, we'll refer to them as *notes*.

To Create a Note

1. Position the cursor to the right of the text to be marked with a note number.

2. Choose Insert ➤ Footnote or Insert ➤ Endnote, then choose Create.

3. Type the text of your note.

4. Choose Close from the feature bar when you are finished.

To Edit a Note

1. Choose Insert ➤ Footnote or Insert ➤ Endnote and then Edit. Or double-click the hidden [Footnote] or [Endnote] code on Reveal Codes.

2. Enter the number, character, or letter of the note you want to edit. Then click OK or press ↵.

3. Edit the note.

4. Choose Close when you are finished.

To Delete a Note

1. Turn on Reveal Codes (Alt+F3) and locate the hidden code for the note you want to delete.

2. Drag that code out of Reveal Codes into the document window.

To Customize Notes

1. Move the cursor so it's before the first note that you want to customize.

2. Choose Insert ➤ Footnote or Insert ➤ Endnote, then choose New Number if you want to renumber the notes or Options if you want to change the appearance or over-all numbering scheme. If you're customizing Endnotes, you can also choose Placement to determine where the end notes will appear in your document.

NOTES WordPerfect automatically numbers and for-mats notes and places them in your document. Notes in Master Documents are numbered as if you were using one large document.

Notes are not visible on the screen when you're using Draft view.

 **SEE ALSO** *Reveal Codes*

FORCE PAGE

Use this feature to force a page to start on an odd or even page number.

To Force an Odd/Even Page

1. Move the cursor to the top of the page that you want to ensure is odd- or even-numbered.

2. Choose Format ➤ Page ➤ Force Page, then choose whichever option is appropriate. Choose OK to return to the document window.

 **SEE ALSO** *Page Breaks*

GENERATE

Generate compiles tables of contents, tables of authorities, indexes, lists, and cross-references automatically. Before using generate, you must mark appropriate entries in your document.

To Generate Reference
Tables, Indexes, and Lists

1. Choose Tools ➤ Generate (Ctrl+F9), or click the Generate
    button in the bar feature (if it is available). If you wish,
    choose Options, then select or clear Save Subdocuments
    and/or Build Hypertext Links and choose OK.

2. Choose OK.

NOTES   Once you've started Generate, a screen message
keeps you informed of its progress.

SEE ALSO   *Cross-Reference, Index, Lists, Master Document, Table of Authorities, Table of Contents*

GO TO

Go To lets you move the cursor to a specific position in a document,
a specific newspaper or parallel column, a cell in a table, or a position within selected text.

To Use Go To

1. Choose Edit ➤ Go To (Ctrl+G).

2. Choose the Position you want to move to or enter a
    Page Number, Bookmark, or Table and Cell/Range,
    then choose OK.

 **SEE ALSO**   Columns, Find, Selecting Text, *Tables*

GRAMMATIK

Grammatik (rhymes with *dramatic)* is a utility that checks the grammar, spelling, and writing style of WordPerfect documents. Grammatik was completely overhauled for version 6.1.

To Start Grammatik

1. Move the cursor to where you want to start checking
grammar, or select the text you want to check.

2. Choose Tools ➤ Grammatik (Alt+Shift+F1), or click the
Grammatik button in the toolbar. Grammatik usually
starts checking immediately. If you want to use the standard options, skip to step 4.

3. If you wish, choose additional options from the dialog box
menus. You can choose the amount of text to check
(Check), the writing style to check against (Preferences),
and various "environmental" options (see *Options* below).
You can also select and update dictionaries
(Dictionaries).

4. When you're ready to start checking, choose the Start button (if necessary). When Grammatik finds an error (or
what it thinks is an error), it displays a message indicating
the type of error. You can then:

- Drag the Grammatik window by its title bar to some
other area of the screen (if you can't see the error in
your document).

- Click in the document window and make your changes
immediately. Then click the Resume button.

- Choose Skip Once to leave the selected text unchanged and continue with the next problem.

- Choose Skip Always to ignore this problem in the selected text and all future text during this checking session.

- Highlight a word in the Replacements list and choose Replace to replace the selected word in your document with the highlighted word in the Replacements list.

- Choose Add to add the selected word in your document to Grammatik's dictionary, so it won't be counted as a misspelling in the future.

- Choose Undo to undo the most recent change.

- Select a different checking style from the Checking Style drop-down list.

- Choose options from the Rule pop-up list button to turn rules on or off, or mark problems without fixing them.

- Choose options from the View menu to view the parts of speech or a parse tree. For mavens of the mother tongue only!

- Click on any green underlined topic to get Help with that topic.

5. Optionally, choose View ➤ Statistics to view document statistics at any time (though it's probably best to do this after checking is complete). Choose Close after viewing the statistics.

6. When you're done, choose Close to close the Grammatik dialog box.

OPTIONS   The environment options control how Grammatik behaves during a grammar check. Choose Preferences ➤ Environment from the dialog box menus, then select (check) or deselect (clear) the options below:

Provide Spelling Suggestions   Determines whether spelling suggestions appear during proofreading. (Selected by default.)

Show Help Prompts   Determines whether Help prompts appear in the title bar. (Selected by default.)

Prompt Before Automatic Replace Determines whether Grammatik prompts before replacing a word marked in the dictionary as an "auto replacement." (Deselected by default.)

Start Checking Immediately Determines whether Grammatik starts checking grammar immediately. (Selected by default.)

Check Headers, Footers, and Footnotes in WordPerfect Determines whether Grammatik will check these areas of your document. (Deselected by default.)

 **SEE ALSO** *Spell Checker, Thesaurus*

GRAPHICS AND GRAPHICS BOXES

The Graphics and Graphics boxes features let you add pictures and other graphic elements to your document.

To Create a Graphics Box

1. Move the cursor to where you want to put the graphics image.

2. If you want to create graphics boxes by dragging an outline anywhere in your document, select Graphics ➤ Drag To Create (to check that option). If you just want a fixed-sized box to appear at the cursor position, make sure that option is not checked. The "drag to create" setting is remembered until you change it again. (New in version 6.1.)

3. Choose Graphics ➤ Image or click the Image button in the toolbar. If you've selected Drag To Create, click in your document and drag an outline to define the initial size and location for your image.

4. If necessary, use the QuickList and/or Drives and Directories lists to switch to the directory on which the graphics
image is stored.

5. Click the name of the graphics image to insert, then
choose OK.

The image will appear in an Image box.

To Size or Position a Graphics Box

- Use your mouse to drag the box to its new location.

- Click the box once and drag one of its sizing handles until
the box is the desired size.

- For more precise positioning, right-click the box, choose
Position, Size, or Wrap, as appropriate, and define the
box's position, size, and text wrap options.

To Change the Contents of a Graphics Box

1. Right-click the box and choose Content, then:

- To put a graphic image into the box, click the button
next to the Filename text box and choose the drive,
directory, and file name of the graphic image to insert.
Then select OK.

- To put text or a table into the box, choose Text from the
Content pop-up list, choose Yes to replace the current
contents, then choose Edit. Create your table and/or
type your text. Choose fonts, justification, and other formatting features in the usual manner. Choose Close
from the feature bar when you're done.

- If you want the box to be empty, choose Empty from
the pop-up list next to Content; if necessary, select Yes
to delete the current contents, then choose OK.

To Change the Box Style or Appearance

There are three ways to change the border and the general appearance of a graphics box:

- To change the borders on the current box only, right-click the box, choose Border/Fill, design your border, and choose OK.

- To switch the box to a different box style, right-click the box, choose Style, then highlight the type of box to which you want to convert the current box, and choose OK.

- To change the appearance of all the boxes in a given category (e.g., all the Image boxes or all the User boxes), choose Graphics ➤ Graphics Styles. Select Options, then Setup ➤ Current Document ➤ OK. In the Styles list box, choose the type of box you want to redesign, then choose Edit. Design the box style from the options given, then choose OK and Close to work your way back to the document window.

To Create or Edit a Caption

1. Right-click the box for which you want to create or edit a caption, then:

- To create or edit the text of a caption, select Create Caption or Edit Caption as appropriate, type or edit your caption, then choose Close from the feature bar.

- To change the position, rotation, or style of the caption, choose Caption and use the options that appear in the Box Caption dialog box. Then choose OK.

To Renumber Boxes

Graphics boxes are numbered consecutively throughout the document by box type. When you create a caption for most box types,

the automatic number appears at the start of the caption. To change
the numbering of boxes:

1. Turn on Reveal Codes (Alt+F3) and move the cursor to
just before the hidden code for the first box you want
renumbered.

2. Choose Insert ➤ Other ➤ Counter and highlight the type
of box you want to renumber. (Image, Figure, and OLE
boxes all use the Figure box counter.)

3. Choose Value, enter the new starting number for the
boxes and choose OK or use any of the other available options to increase or decrease the number.

You can also choose Edit from the Counter Numbering
dialog box to switch to some other numbering method
such as letters (A, B, C, D) or roman numerals
(I, II, III, IV).

4. Click OK and Close as necessary to return to the document window.

OPTIONS When you're positioning a graphics box, you can
choose from the following anchor options:

Put Box On Current Page (Page Anchor) Lets you define a
specific place on the page to put the box. Text will flow around
the box.

Put Box In Current Paragraph (Paragraph Anchor) The box
will be attached to its nearest paragraph and will float with
that paragraph. That is, if you insert or delete text above the
paragraph that the box is anchored to, the box will move automatically to stay attached to its neighboring paragraph.

Treat Box As Character (Character Anchor) The box is anchored to its nearest character and moves along with that character as you insert and delete other text.

Place (Horizontal) Positions the box horizontally from a
specified location.

Place (Vertical) Positions the box vertically from a specified location.

NOTES There are ten different types of graphic boxes: Image, Text, Equation, Figure, Table, User, Button, Watermark, Inline Equation, and OLE 2.0. However, all graphic boxes are virtually the same. The type of box you choose only defines the initial appearance of the box and the numbering system to use. For example, your document might contain Figure boxes numbered 1, 2, etc., but it might also contain Table boxes numbered 1, 2, etc.

Instead of right-clicking a box and choosing options from the QuickMenus, you can use buttons on the Graphics Box feature bar. If the feature bar isn't visible, right-click the box and choose Feature Bar.

SEE ALSO *Chart; Draw, Graphics Editor, Graphics Lines and Borders, Styles, Text Art*

GRAPHICS EDITOR

The graphics image editor lets you make changes to existing images in a graphics box.

To Use the Graphics Editor

1. Right-click the graphics box you want to change and choose Image Tools. Or, click the Tools button in the Graphics Box feature bar. The tools palette shown in Figure 4 appears.

2. Make your changes using the available tools, then click in the document window outside the graphics box.

NOTES If the Image Tools palette overlays the graphic image, drag the horizontal bar at the top of the palette to a clear area. To close the Image Tools palette, double-click its upper-left corner or repeat step 1 above.

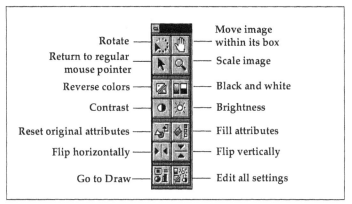

Figure 4: Image Tools Palette

 **SEE ALSO** *Draw, Graphics and Graphics Boxes, Graphics Lines and Borders*

GRAPHICS LINES AND BORDERS

The Graphics Lines command allows you to put graphics lines anywhere in your document. The Border/Fill commands let you add borders and fills to paragraphs, pages, columns, tables, and graphics. Be aware that you can only print graphics lines with a graphics printer.

To Create a Graphics Line

1. Move the cursor to where you want the line to appear.

2. Choose Graphics, then choose either Horizontal Line (Ctrl+F11) for a horizontal line that runs from the left to the right margin, Vertical Line (Ctrl+Shift+F11) for a vertical line that runs from the top to bottom margin, or Custom Line for any other type of horizontal or vertical line.

3. If you chose Custom Line in step 2, you can now define the style, type, position, length, etc., by choosing options from the Create Graphics Line dialog box that appears. Choose OK when you're done.

To Change a Graphics Line

• Click the line so that it has sizing handles, then drag the entire line to a new location or drag just the sizing handles to change the length or thickness of the line.

• Or, double-click the line, or right-click the line and choose Edit Horizontal (or Vertical) Line to get to the Edit Graphics Line dialog box. Choose OK when you're done.

To Delete a Line

Click the line once, then press Delete (Del).

To Add or Delete Borders and Fill

1. Position the cursor in, or select, the area you want to border or fill.

2. Choose the appropriate Border/Fill command:

• For paragraphs, pages, or columns: choose Format, then either Paragraph, Page, or Columns, then choose Border/Fill.

• For tables: right-click the table and choose Lines/Fill, or press Shift+F12, or choose Table ➤ Lines/Fill.

• For graphics: right-click the graphic and choose Border/Fill, or click the Border/Fill button in the Graphics Box feature bar.

3. Complete the dialog box, using the sample picture as a guide.

4. Choose OK.

NOTES   If you select Do Not Print Graphics from the Print dialog box just before printing, the lines won't be printed.

If you choose Options ➤ Print Job Graphically in the Print dialog box just before printing, the graphics lines will not print through any graphics boxes that they intersect.

If you have trouble selecting the graphics line with the mouse, zoom in to 200% and then click it.

SEE ALSO   *Headers, Footers, and Watermarks; Print; Zoom*

HEADERS, FOOTERS, AND WATERMARKS

You can print *repeating elements* at the top (headers), bottom (footers), or behind the text (watermarks) of every page, odd pages only, or even pages only. Watermarks are pale gray and are covered by the text and graphics on a page.

To Create or Edit a Repeating Element

1.   Move the cursor to the top of the page where the repeating element should take effect.

2.   To create or edit a header or footer, choose Format ➤ Header/Footer. To create or edit a watermark, choose Format Watermark.

3.   Choose Header A, Header B, Footer A, Footer B, Watermark A, or Watermark B.

4.   Choose Create or Edit.

5.   Type or edit the header, footer, or watermark and choose any options you want (see *Notes* and *Options*, below).

6. Choose Close on the feature bar to return to the document window.

To Discontinue a Repeating Element

1. Position the cursor on the page where you want to discontinue the repeating element.

2. Choose Format ➤ Header/Footer or Format ➤ Watermark.

3. Choose Header A, Header B, Footer A, Footer B, Watermark A, or Watermark B.

4. Choose Discontinue.

OPTIONS These options are available on the Header/Footer or Watermark feature bar:

Close Closes the editing window and hides the feature bar.

Distance Controls the distance between the text and repeating element. (Headers and footers only.)

File Inserts a file at the cursor position. (Watermarks only.)

Image Inserts a graphics image at the cursor position. (Watermarks only.)

Line Inserts a horizontal or vertical line at the cursor position. (Headers and footers only.)

Next Edits the next repeating element of the same type (e.g., the next Header A).

Number Inserts a page, secondary page, chapter, or volume number at the cursor position. (Headers and footers only.)

Pages Places the repeating element on Odd Pages, Even Pages, or Every Page (default).

Previous Edits the previous repeating element of the same type (e.g., the previous Header A).

Shading Controls the shading for text and images. (Water mark only.)

NOTES You can define up to two headers (A and B), two footers (A and B), and two watermarks (A and B) per document page to use at any time, and you can change them as needed. A repeating element will remain in effect until you define a different repeating element, suppress it (see *Suppress*), discontinue it, or delete it.

WordPerfect automatically adds an extra line after a header and before a footer.

Repeating elements may contain up to one page of text.

Repeating elements appear in Page or Two-Page view, but not in Draft view.

To delete a repeating element, turn on Reveal Codes (Alt+F3) and drag the appropriate [Header], [Footer], or [Watermark] code into the document window.

To edit a repeating element quickly, turn on Reveal Codes (Alt+F3) and double-click the appropriate [Header], [Footer], or [Watermark] code. To quickly edit headers and footers in Page view (View ➤ Page), click in the header or footer area of the page, make your changes, and then click in the main document area. In Page view, you can also right-click the header or footer area on the page and choose Header/Footer or Watermark from the QuickMenu.

While editing a repeating element, you can use all the usual features of WordPerfect, including graphics, fonts, Spell Checker, Thesaurus, Insert ➤ Date, and Insert ➤ Other, as well as buttons in the feature bar (see *Options*, above).

SEE ALSO *Delay Codes, Page Numbering, Suppress*

HELP

Like all Windows applications, WordPerfect provides both general and context-sensitive help. General help explains basic WordPerfect tasks. Context-sensitive help pertains to the task you're doing or to a specific region of the screen. Help was enhanced significantly in version 6.1.

To Access Help

Choose options from the Help menu, press F1, click the Help button (if it's available in a dialog box), or press Shift+F1 and click on an area of the screen. The results of pressing F1 depend on what was active when you pressed it:

- From a document window, the Help contents appear.

- From the Help window, information about how to use Help appears.

- From active menu items, dialog boxes, or special windows (such as Spell Checker), specific information about the item appears.

To Find Help Topics

Use any method below to find information on a topic:

- Choose Help ➤ Contents from the menu bar, then click the Help section you want.

- Choose Help ➤ Search For Help On from the menu bar, or click the Search button while in a Help window. Type a word or scroll to locate the topic, then double-click the topic. In the lower window, scroll to the topic you want, then double-click it.

- Choose Help ➤ How Do I from the menu bar. Click the appropriate book icon to reveal (or close) a list of related topics. Keep on clicking until you find the topic you want. To expand or close all the books quickly, click the Open Books or Close Books icons, respectively. (New in version 6.1.)

- Choose a *jump* word, indicated by colored or underlined text or as a graphic, from the help text to look up topics related to the current one.

To Exit Help

- Press Esc, or choose File ➤ Exit, or double-click the Help window's Control-menu box, or click the Help window's Close button.

To Print Help Information

Open the Help window you want to print, then…

1. Choose File ➤ Print Setup (if necessary), set the options you need, and choose OK.

2. Choose File ➤ Print Topic to print the current topic, or File ➤ Print Topics to print groups of related topics or all topics.

NOTES   To find out more about macros, choose Help ➤ Macros from the menu bar.

Three of WordPerfect's Help menu options will get you up and running fast. These are Help ➤ Coaches, Help ➤ Upgrade Expert and Help ➤ Tutorial, all available from the WordPerfect menu bar.

Help ➤ Coaches takes you through an actual WordPerfect operation step by step. To use Coaches, position the cursor where you want the operation to begin, choose Help ➤ Coaches, select the option you want, and follow the prompts on the screen.

Help ➤ Upgrade Expert helps you move from another word processor to WordPerfect 6, or to learn WordPerfect's top features quickly. Like Coaches, the Upgrade Expert can take you through an operation step by step.

Help ➤ Tutorial runs an interactive tutorial that shows you how to use basic WordPerfect features. The *Examples* entry in the Help Contents shows you pictures of what you can do in WordPerfect and explains how to do it.

Help ➤ About WordPerfect displays the current version of Word-Perfect, the license number, and other information.

 **SEE ALSO** *Your WordPerfect 6.1 for Windows manual*

HIDDEN TEXT

The Hidden Text feature prevents selected text from being displayed on the screen or printed.

To Hide Text

1. Select the text, fonts, attributes, lines, graphics, or other information that you want to hide.

2. Choose Format ➤ Font (or press F9).

3. Select (check) Hidden under Appearance in the Font dialog box.

4. Choose OK.

To Display or Hide Hidden Text

Choose View ➤ Hidden Text to switch between displaying or hiding hidden text. When hidden text is visible, you can edit and print it as you would any normal text.

To Delete Hidden Text

Choose View ➤ Reveal Codes (Alt+F3), then delete the [Hidden] code at the beginning or end of the hidden text.

NOTES Hidden text is useful for writing notes to yourself or hiding information that you might want to display and print later.

When hidden text is visible, WordPerfect treats it like any other information in your document.

You can hide any text, graphics, fonts, or codes between the [Hidden] codes.

 **SEE ALSO**   *Comment, Font*

HIDE BARS

This command lets you hide WordPerfect's toolbar, power bar, ruler bar, scroll bar, status bar, and menu bar in a single step.

To Hide All the Bars

Choose View ➤ Hide Bars or press Alt+Shift+F5, then choose OK.

To Redisplay the Bars

Press Esc or Alt+Shift+F5. Or, press Alt+V, then choose Hide Bars.

 **NOTES**   To display or hide individual bars, choose any of the following options from the View menu: Toolbar, Power Bar, Ruler Bar (Alt+Shift+F3), or Status Bar. All these options are toggles: when selected (checked), the bar is visible; when deselected, the bar is hidden.

You can also hide a bar by right-clicking the bar and choosing Hide...Bar from the QuickMenu.

 **SEE ALSO**   *Menus, Power Bar, Ruler, Status Bar, Toolbar*

HYPERTEXT

Hypertext is a *hot spot* that you put into your documents. The hot spot, which is either a section of colored, underlined text (like the *jump words* in Help) or a command button, will perform some action when clicked. For example, clicking on a hot spot could open a document, jump to a bookmark, or do anything else a macro can do.

Hypertext features are available when the Hypertext feature bar is visible.

To Display or Hide the Hypertext Feature Bar

- To display the feature bar, choose Tools ➤ Hypertext.

- To hide the feature bar, choose the Close button in the feature bar.

To Create or Change a Hypertext Hot Spot

1. Create the WordPerfect document, bookmark, or macro you want the hot spot to jump *to*.

2. If you're creating hypertext, select the text you want to jump *from*. If you're changing hypertext, move the cursor just past the underlined text or button.

3. Display the Hypertext feature bar.

4. Click the Create or Edit button in the feature bar.

5. Select an action and fill in the text box. Your options are Go To Bookmark, Go To Other Document and Bookmark, and Run Macro.

6. Select an appearance, either Text or Button.

7. Choose OK.

To Jump to and from Hypertext

1. Display the Hypertext feature bar and move the cursor to the hypertext link you want to jump from.

2. If the Activate button is visible, click it. The button changes to Deactivate.

3. Click the link you are jumping from. The cursor moves to the bookmark or document, or the macro runs.

4. Choose the Back button on the feature bar to return to the original hypertext text or button.

5. Choose the Next button in the feature bar to jump to the next link. Choose the Previous button to move to the previous link.

To Edit the Hypertext Text or Button

1. Display the Hypertext feature bar.

2. Make sure the Activate/Deactivate button says Activate.

3. Edit the text as if it were normal text, or edit the button as you would any graphic box.

4. When you're done making changes, click the Activate button in the feature bar (its name changes back to Deactivate).

To Delete Hypertext

1. Display the Hypertext feature bar.

2. Position the cursor inside the hypertext (for text), or just before the hypertext button. To make this easier, click the Next or Previous button in the Hypertext feature bar, or turn on Reveal Codes (Alt+F3).

3. Click the Delete button in the feature bar. (Choose Edit ➤ Undo or press Ctrl+Z immediately if you want to recover deleted hypertext.)

To Generate Hypertext Links

You can build hypertext links when you generate lists for a master document.

1. Choose Tools ➤ Generate or press Ctrl+F9, then choose Options.

2. Select (check) Build Hypertext Links to build the links; deselect the option to generate the lists without building links first (this will be faster). Choose OK twice to start generating the lists.

NOTES To deactivate hypertext, click the Deactivate button in the feature bar. You must deactivate hypertext before you can change the underlined text or appearance of the button at the hot spot.

To activate hypertext, click the Activate button in the feature bar.

If hypertext is active, you can jump to a hot spot by clicking on it, even if the Hypertext feature bar isn't visible. To jump back, however, you'll need to display the Hypertext feature bar and click the Back button.

SEE ALSO *Bookmark, Feature Bar, Generate, Graphics and Graphics Boxes, List, Macros, Sound*

HYPHENATION

Hyphenation adds a smoother, more professional look to your document by automatically hyphenating words at the end of lines that would contain too much white space if the whole word was wrapped. You can hyphenate words manually or let WordPerfect do it for you.

To Turn Automatic Hyphenation On and Off

1. Position the cursor where you want to turn hyphenation on or off.

2. Choose Format ➤ Line ➤ Hyphenation.

3. Select (check) Hyphenation On to turn hyphenation on. Deselect Hyphenation On to turn hyphenation off.

4. Choose OK.

To Respond to Hyphenation Prompts

If WordPerfect needs your help during automatic hyphenation, the word that needs hyphenation will appear in the Position Hyphen dialog box. Position the hyphen in the word by clicking the mouse where you want the hyphen to appear, or by using the ← and → keys. Then click Insert Hyphen.

If you prefer not to insert a hyphen when prompted for hyphenation help, you can choose other options in the Position Hyphen dialog box:

• To prevent the word from being hyphenated now or later and to wrap the word to the next line, choose Ignore Word.

• To stop hyphenating words temporarily, choose Suspend Hyphenation.

• To insert a hyphenation soft return instead of a hyphen at the hyphenation point, choose Hyphenation SRt.

• To insert a space instead of a hyphen at the hyphenation point, choose Insert Space.

To Hyphenate Manually

1. Position the cursor where you want the character or code to appear.

2. Type the character or code (if it's available on the keyboard), or choose Format ➤ Line ➤ Other codes (see *Table II*).

Table II: A Summary of Hyphens and Dashes

HYPHEN CHARACTER AND CODE	DESCRIPTION	KEYSTROKE*
Hyphen [- Hyphen]	Permanent (-) hyphen used to break two words at the end of a line. Use for words that normally include hyphens, such as *father-in-law*.	
Soft hyphen [- Soft Hyphen]	Temporary hyphen that breaks a word only when necessary (WordPerfect uses this during automatic hyphenation).	Ctrl+Shift+-
Hard hyphen -	A dash (-) that's never separated at the end of a line. Use to insert a hyphen in words that shouldn't break at the end of a line, such as *tip-top*.	Ctrl+-
En dash [–:4,33]	A dash (–) that's never separated at the end of a line.	Ctrl+W **n-**
Em dash [—:4,34]	A dash (—) that's never separated at the end of a line.	Ctrl+W **m-**
Hyphenation soft return [Hyph SRt]	Breaks words at a certain place when hyphenation is needed, but doesn't display a hyphen.	Choose Format ➤ Line ➤ Other Codes ➤ Hyphenation Soft Return↵
Ignore Word [Cancel Hyph]	Wraps the entire word to the next line and prevents future hyphenation.	Ctrl+/

*NOTE: *If you can't remember which character produces the hyphenation code, choose Format*➤ *Line * ➤ *Other Codes, select the character you want from the dialog box, and press * ↵.

3. If necessary, select a hyphenation option from the Other Codes dialog box and choose Insert.

Table II lists various hyphenation characters, codes, and information on how to type them into a word.

To Set the Hyphenation Zone

WordPerfect uses the hyphenation zone to decide when to break a word during automatic hyphenation. There are two zones, one on each side of the right margin. Hyphenation zones are measured as a percentage of the line length. With hyphenation on, WordPerfect hyphenates words that start before the left zone and extend past the right zone.

1. Position the cursor where you want to change the hyphenation zone.

2. Choose Format ➤ Line ➤ Hyphenation.

3. Enter the percentage of line length to use for the Left and Right hyphenation zones. Set a wide zone to hyphenate fewer words or a narrow zone to hyphenate more words.

4. Choose OK.

To Choose Hyphenation Environment Settings

Customize hyphenation by changing Environment Preferences settings.

1. Choose Edit ➤ Preferences and double-click Environment.

2. Choose any of the options below.

- To control how often you're prompted during automatic hyphenation, choose Hyphenation Prompt and select one of these options: Always (prompts when a word needs hyphenation); Never (never prompts for help; the entire word is wrapped to the next line if its hyphenation isn't found); When Required (prompts only if a word's hyphenation isn't found).

- To turn the beep on when WordPerfect needs hyphenation help, select (check) Hyphenation in the Beep On area. To turn off the beep, deselect Hyphenation.

3.   Choose OK, then Close.

 NOTES   When hyphenation is off, WordPerfect wraps (moves) a word to the next line when the word extends beyond the right margin. When hyphenation is on, WordPerfect will hyphenate words as you type or scroll through existing text.

SEE ALSO   *Justification, Preferences*

INDENT

WordPerfect provides several ways to indent paragraphs or blocks of text.

To Indent a Paragraph

1.   Place the cursor where the indent should start. You can indent at existing text or where you're about to type.

2.   Press an indent key or choose one of the indent options listed below:

- To indent the *first line* of a paragraph, press Tab.

- To indent the *left margin,* press F7, choose Format ➤ Paragraph ➤ Indent, or click the Indent button on the WordPerfect Toolbar.

- To indent the *left and right margins* by an equal amount, press Ctrl+Shift+F7, choose Format ➤ Paragraph ➤ Double Indent.

- To insert a *hanging indent*, press Ctrl+F7 or choose For̲mat ➤ P̲aragraph ➤ H̲anging Indent. A hanging indent keeps the first line in a paragraph flush with the left margin while indenting the remaining lines.

- To insert a *margin release*, choose Fo̲rmat ➤ P̲aragraph ➤ Back T̲ab or press Shift+Tab. A margin release moves the cursor to the left by one tab stop. If the cursor is at the start of an indented line, that line returns to the left margin (like a hanging indent).

3. If necessary, type the paragraph and press ↵.

To Create Numbered or Bulleted Indented Lists

You can create numbered or bulleted lists in which the text following the item number or bullet is indented (like lists in this book).

1. Move the cursor to where the list should begin.

2. Create your list as follows:

- To create a list "manually," type the item number (e.g., 1.) or a bullet character (e.g., press Ctrl+W, type **, and press ↵). Press F7 or Ctrl+Shift+F7 to indent or double-indent. Type the text for the list item, then press ↵ once or twice. Repeat these steps as needed.

- To create an automatic numbered or bulleted list, see the Bullets and Numbers entry.

- To create an outline, see the Outline entry.

NOTES Indentation is based on the current tab settings. Each time you indent, the indentation will move to the next tab stop.

When typing new text, indentation remains in effect until you press ↵ or insert a page break (Ctrl+↵ or Ctrl+Shift +↵ or column break (Ctrl+↵).

The Fo̲rmat ➤ P̲aragraph ➤ F̲ormat commands and the ruler provide another way to indent the left and right margin in paragraphs. (See *Paragraph* and *Ruler.*)

WordPerfect can automatically generate various lists such as lists of captioned figures. (*See List.*)

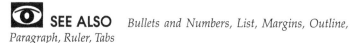 **SEE ALSO** *Bullets and Numbers, List, Margins, Outline, Paragraph, Ruler, Tabs*

INDEX

You can create an index for your document using WordPerfect's Index feature. This involves three basic steps. First, create a concordance file or mark index entries in your document. Second, define the index location and appearance. Third, generate the index.

Index features are available when the Index feature bar is visible.

To Display or Close the Index Feature Bar

- To display the feature bar, choose Tools ➤ Index.

- To hide the feature bar, choose the Close button in the feature bar.

To Create a Concordance File

A concordance file contains all the words and phrases that you want included in the index. When you define the index, you can have WordPerfect use the concordance file only or use the concordance file along with marked text within the document.

1. Open a blank document window by pressing Ctrl +N or clicking the New Blank Document button on the toolbar.

2. Type a word or phrase to include in the index and press ⏎. Repeat this step for each word or phrase you want to index.

3. Sort the list alphabetically to speed up index generation. Choose Tools ➤ Sort (Alt+F9), specify the sort keys and options, and choose Sort.

4. Save the concordance file. Choose File ➤ Save (Ctrl+S) or click the Save button on the toolbar, type a file name, and choose OK.

WordPerfect will generate an index entry whenever a phrase in the document *exactly* matches a phrase in the concordance file. Uppercase and lowercase entries (e.g., "TREES" and "trees") are treated the same.

To Mark Index Entries within a Document

1. Display the Index feature bar.

2. Select the word or phrase you want to index. (You can choose Edit ➤ Find and Replace or press F2 to locate words and phrases quickly.)

3. To specify the heading for this entry, click the Heading drop-down list button in the feature bar. The selected text will appear in the list. You can edit this if you wish, or select an existing heading from the list.

4. To specify the subheading for this entry (optional), click the Subheading drop-down list button. The selected text will appear in the list. You can edit this if you wish, or select an existing subheading from the list.

5. Click the Mark button in the feature bar.

6. Repeat steps 3–5 until you've entered and marked all the headings and subheadings for the selected text.

To mark additional entries in your document, repeat steps 2–6 for each word or phrase.

To Define the Index
Location and Page Numbering Style

1. Move the cursor to where you want the index to appear (usually at the end of your document).

2. Optionally, press Ctrl+↵ (or Ctrl+Shift+↵ if you are working in columns) to insert a page break.

3. Optionally, type a title for the index and press ↵.

4. Display the Index feature bar.

5. Click the <u>D</u>efine button in the feature bar. The Define Index dialog box appears.

6. Choose any appearance options you want (see Options, below).

7. If you're using a concordance file, enter its name into the <u>F</u>ile-name text box, or use the file button to locate the file.

8. Choose OK.

To Generate an Index

1. Display the Index feature bar.

2. Click the <u>G</u>enerate button in the feature bar or press Ctrl+F9.

3. Choose OK.

OPTIONS   The following options in the Define Index dialog box control the appearance of index entries.

Position   Lets you define where the page number appears with respect to the text of the index entry.

Page Numbering   Lets you define the format of the page number.

Use Dash To Show Consecutive Pages   When selected (checked), a dash indicates consecutive page numbers. When deselected, each page number in a range is listed separately.

Change   Lets you change the style of the heading and sub-heading entries.

NOTES   You can mark the word or phrase being indexed as a heading or as both a heading and subheading.

The word or phrase being indexed need not match its heading or subheading. For example, in a book about wildlife observation, you might select the phrase "Identifying Tracks." Then, after choosing Heading on the feature bar, you could change the phrase to "Tracks, Identifying." Or, enter "Tracks" as the Heading and "Identifying" as the subheading.

To delete an index entry in the document, choose View ➤ Reveal Codes (Alt+F3) and delete the appropriate [Index] code.

See the QuickFinder entry to learn about another type of index that can instantly show you which files contain a particular word or phrase.

Concordance file entries are automatically used as index headings. For more control over the headings and subheadings, you can mark concordance file entries as explained in "To Mark Index Entries within a Document" above.

👁 **SEE ALSO** *Find, Generate, List, Master Document, Page Numbering, QuickFinder, Sorting and Selecting, Styles, Table of Authorities, Table of Contents*

INITIAL CODES STYLE

The initial codes style is WordPerfect's default setting for a document's content and appearance.

To Change the Initial Codes Style for a Document

1. Choose Format ➤ Document ➤ Initial Codes Style. The Styles Editor dialog box appears.

2. In the Contents box, enter all the text, formatting codes, graphics, and other features you want to predefine. You can type text, use the Styles Editor pull-down menus, or press shortcut keys as needed. See the Styles entry for details.

3. Select (check) the Use As Default checkbox if you want to change the initial codes style for all subsequent documents.

4.   Choose OK when you're done.

NOTES   You can define initial codes for nearly every WordPerfect feature (unavailable options will be grayed out in the menus).

The [Open Style:InitialStyle] code for the initial codes style always appears in the Reveal Codes screen at the start of each document.

You can also change the initial codes style by turning on Reveal Codes (Alt+F3) and double-clicking the [Open Style:InitialStyle] code.

You can define an initial font to override a font in the initial codes style. (See the Initial Font entry.)

Formatting codes entered into the document itself override all initial codes style and initial font settings.

You can also use templates to predefine the look of a document and to determine WordPerfect's behavior and available features. See the Template entry for more information.

If you want to update the Initial Codes Style for use in other documents, use the Styles feature (see the Styles entry). You can update the system style named "InitialStyle" and save your changes to the current document, default template, additional objects template, or a style library file.

SEE ALSO   *Codes, Font, Initial Font, Styles, Template*

INITIAL FONT

The initial font for a document overrides any font specified in the initial codes style (see *Initial Codes Style*).

To Choose an Initial Font

1. Choose Format ➤ Document ➤ Initial Font, or press F9 and choose Initial Font.

2. Choose the font face, font style, and font size as appropriate.

3. Optionally, select the Set As Printer Initial Font checkbox.

4. Choose OK.

 NOTES   Font changes that you make within your document will override the initial font and the initial codes style.

SEE ALSO   *Font, Font Setup, Initial Codes Style*

INSERT/TYPEOVER

In Insert mode, new text, blank lines, and most codes you type are inserted into existing text at the cursor position. In Typeover mode, new text replaces existing text, but codes are left intact.

To Switch between Modes

Press the Insert key or double-click the Insert or Typeover button in the Status bar.

To Insert Text

In general, follow these steps to insert text or a formatting code:

1. Move the cursor where text should appear or the code should take effect, or select a block of text.

2. Type the text, or insert the code using the pull-down menus or keyboard shortcuts.

NOTES   In Typeover mode, pressing Backspace deletes existing text and replaces it with blank spaces (one space for each press of the key). You can press Ctrl+Shift+Z to undelete the text.

Here are some more details about Insert mode:

- If you don't select text before typing, *new text or unpaired codes* will appear at the cursor position.

- If you select text before typing, new text will replace the selected text.

- If you select text before choosing a formatting code, you'll insert paired codes around the selected text.

- To insert blank lines into existing text. move the cursor to the left edge of the line that should appear below the blank lines (or move it to the end of the line that should appear above the blank lines). Press ↵ once for each blank line you want to insert.

- To insert a blank line as you type, press ↵ twice at the end of the line. (Continue pressing ↵ to add more blank lines.)

- To insert paired formatting codes as you type, choose the pull-down menu option for the paired code or press its shortcut key, and then type the text. To move beyond the paired codes, press →, choose the menu option, or press the shortcut key again.

- To insert characters from the WordPerfect character sets, choose Insert ➤ Character or press Ctrl+W.

- To insert special formatting codes (hard tabs, hard tabs with dot leaders, hyphenation codes, hard spaces, and End Centering/Alignment codes), choose Layout ➤ Line ➤ Other Codes, select the code you want, then choose Insert. Shortcut keys are also available for most of these codes.

- To insert bullets and numbers followed by an indent, choose Insert ➤ Bullets & Numbers or press Ctrl+Shift+B.

SEE ALSO *Bullets and Numbers, Characters, Cursor, Document Window, Font, Hyphenation, Macros, Selecting Text, Spaces (Hard and Soft), Tabs, Undelete*

INSTALL

You must install WordPerfect for Windows before you can use it.

To Install WordPerfect for Windows

1. Start Windows in the usual manner (type **win** and press ↵ at the DOS prompt).

2. Insert the WordPerfect for Windows disk labeled "Setup" in drive A or drive B (depending on the size of the diskettes).

3. If you're using Windows 95, choose Start ➤ Run. If you're using Windows 3.x, choose File ➤ Run from Program Manager's menu bar.

4. Type **a:\setup** (if the Install 1 disk is in drive A) or **b:\setup** (if the Install 1 disk is in drive B).

5. Choose Install to start the installation program.

6. Type your Name, Company, and Serial Number into the appropriate text boxes in the Registration Information dialog box, then choose Continue.

7. In the Installation Type dialog box, choose the type of installation you want (see Options, below).

8. Choose buttons and fill in dialog boxes according to the options you chose in step 7. (If you need to cancel the installation at any time, choose Cancel and Exit Setup until you return to Windows.)

9. To start the installation, choose Start Installation or OK (depending on your choice in step 7).

10. Assuming you chose to start the installation, feed in new disks and provide other information when prompted.

OPTIONS You'll find the following installation options in the Installation Type dialog box:

Standard Installs all WordPerfect for Windows files to a hard drive that you select. Requires about 30 MB of disk space.

Custom Lets you choose the source and destination for the WordPerfect for Windows files, and which files to install.

Network Installs WordPerfect for Windows for use on a network server or workstation.

Minimum Installs a small WordPerfect system (about 11 MB), which doesn't include Spell Checker, Thesaurus, QuickFinder, WP Draw, macros, graphic files, learning files, help files, and other nonessential files. This is helpful if you're short on hard disk space. If more space becomes available later, you can use the Custom installation to add the missing modules.

Options Lets you view the README files for late-breaking news and product information that didn't make it into the WordPerfect manuals, and lets you install new or updated WordPerfect printer files, conversion drivers, TrueType fonts, and utilities.

To Start WordPerfect for Windows

1. If you're using Windows 95, choose Start ➤ Programs. Choose the WordPerfect 6.1 folder, then click the WP-WIN 6.1 icon. Skip the steps that follow.

2. If you're using Windows 3.x, first make sure to start Windows. If you're at the C:\> prompt type win ↵ to switch from DOS to Windows.

3. In Program Manager, double-click the WPWin 6.1 group icon, then double-click the WPWin 6.1 application icon.

⊙ **SEE ALSO** *Your WordPerfect 6.1 for Windows User's Guide and Getting Started booklet*

JUSTIFICATION

Justification aligns text between margins. You can justify all text, selected text, or a single line.

To Justify All or Selected Text

1. Move the cursor where the new setting should take effect, or select a block of text.

2. Choose an option from the For̲mat ➤ J̲ustification menu, or press the equivalent shortcut key, or select options from the Justification button on the power bar. (See *Options*, below.)

To Center or Right-Justify a Single Line

1. Position the cursor at the start of an existing line or where you're about to type a new line.

2. Choose For̲mat ➤ L̲ine, then either C̲enter or F̲lush Right. Or press Shift+F7 (Center) or Alt+F7 (Flush Right). To insert a dot leader in front of centered or right-aligned text, repeat this step.

3. If necessary, type the line and press ↵. (Pressing ↵ turns off justification for the line.)

OPTIONS   You can choose the following justification options from the For̲mat ➤ J̲ustification menu or the power bar's Justification button:

Left (Ctrl+L) Aligns text against the left margin, leaving the right margin ragged (uneven).

Right (Ctrl+R) Aligns text against the right margin, leaving the left margin ragged.

Center (Ctrl+E) Centers text between margins.

Full   (Ctrl+J) Aligns text evenly against both the left and right margins. WordPerfect expands or compresses spaces between words to even out the line, according to the Word Spacing Justification Limits. (See Typesetting.)

All   Similar to Full justification. However, this option also spreads short lines of text to touch the right margin.

NOTES   Document justification is ignored in tables. The position of the table on the page is determined by the options in the Alignment area of the Table's Format dialog box (Table ➤ Format or Ctrl+F12).

SEE ALSO   *Center, Hyphenation, Initial Codes Style, Power Bar, Tables, Typesetting*

KEEP TEXT TOGETHER

This feature offers three ways to keep your text together—Block Protect, Widow/Orphan, and Conditional End of Page. Use it to prevent text separation across page breaks, to activate widow and orphan protection at first and last lines of paragraphs, and to keep a specific number of lines together.

To Keep Text Together

1.   Position the cursor or select the text as follows:

- For widow/orphan protection or conditional end of page, position the cursor where you want the feature to take effect.

- For block protection, select the text you want to keep together.

2.   Choose Format ➤ Page ➤ Keep Text Together.

3. To turn a feature on, select (check) it in the dialog box. To turn the feature off, deselect it.

4. If you selected Number Of Lines To Keep Together in step 3, specify the number of lines you want to keep together. Be sure to include lines of text and any blank lines in between.

5. Choose OK or press ↵.

NOTES Block protect prevents a passage of text, such as a quotation, sidebar, or columnar table, from being split across two pages. Block protect places paired [Block Pro] codes around a protected block of text. Any changes that you make to the protected block, including new or deleted lines, will still keep the entire block protected.

SEE ALSO *Selecting Text*

KERNING

The process of adjusting the white space between pairs of letters automatically or manually is called *kerning*.

To Kern Letters Automatically

1. Move the cursor to where automatic kerning should start (or end), or select a block of text.

2. Choose Format ➤ Typesetting ➤ Word/Letterspacing.

3. To turn automatic kerning on, select (check) Automatic Kerning. To turn it off, deselect the option.

4. Choose OK.

To Kern Letters Manually

1. Move the cursor between the two letters you wish to adjust.

2. Choose Format ➤ Typesetting ➤ Manual Kerning. If necessary, move the Manual Kerning dialog box so that you can see the letters as you're kerning.

3. Optionally, use the Units Of Measure drop-down list button to select a unit of measure.

4. In the Amount text box, use the spin buttons to increase or decrease the amount of space between the letters. (With each click of a spin button, the letters will move in the document window.)

5. Choose OK.

👁 **SEE ALSO** *Typesetting*

KICKOFF

KickOff starts any application at a specified time and at a repeat interval. Although KickOff is specially designed to automate updates to QuickFinder indexes, you can use it to launch any program at a specified time.

To Use KickOff

1. Double-click the Kickoff icon in the WPWin 6.1 group window in Program Manager. The KickOff dialog box appears. If KickOff is set to start minimized, use the Task List (Ctrl+Esc) or press Alt+Tab to view the dialog box.

2. You can do any of these tasks:

- To *add a new event,* choose Add (see "To Add an Event" below).

- To *change settings for an event,* highlight the event in the Events list and choose Edit (or double-click the event you want to change). Edit the event as desired, then choose OK.

- To *delete an event,* highlight the event in the Events list, choose Remove, then choose Yes to confirm the deletion.

- To *customize* KickOff, choose Setup. Select or deselect the options you want, then choose OK. The Setup options are Start KickOff Minimized, Remove Events Upon Completion, Disable Old Events On Startup, and Write Launch Errors To A Log File.

3. When you're done using KickOff, minimize it or choose Close. (Events will launch only when KickOff is running, not when it's closed.)

To Add an Event

1. Choose Add from the KickOff dialog box.

2. Enter the full command line for the program you want to run, or use the Browse button to locate the program. For example, to run the Windows calendar, you'd type **c:\windows\calendar.exe.**

3. Enter the starting Date for the event.

4. Enter the starting Time and choose the appropriate AM or PM setting.

5. To launch the program at regular intervals, enter the number of Days, or Hrs:Mins (hours and minutes), or both to repeat the launch.

6. To run the application minimized, select (check) Run Minimized.

7. To temporarily prevent the program from launching from KickOff, select (check) D̲isable. (The program will not launch automatically until you clear the check box.)

8. Choose OK.

To Launch QuickFinder from KickOff

Follow the steps above for adding an event (don't check D̲isable in step 7). Use the following command line in step 2:

c:\office\shared\wpc20\qfwin20.exe *options*

Replace *options* with any of the following:

/ra   Rebuilds all indexes listed in the QuickFinder Index Names list box.

/r-*long name*   Rebuilds only the index specified by *long name*

/ia   Updates all indexes with new or modified files

/i-*long name*   Updates the index specified by *long name* with new or modified files

To specify more than one index name, separate each name by a comma and a space, as in

c:\office\shared\wpc20\qfwin20.exe\r-document, customer

 **SEE ALSO**   *QuickFinder*

LABELS

This feature makes it easy to set up and print mailing labels, file folder labels, diskette labels, and index cards.

To Select a Label Format

1. If necessary, choose File ➤ Print ➤ Select and select the printer that you want to use with the labels. Return to the document window.

2. Move the cursor to where the new setting should take effect, or select a block of text.

3. Choose Format ➤ Labels. The Labels dialog box opens.

4. Optionally, choose Change to select a different file of label formats.

5. Optionally, choose Laser, Tractor-Fed, or Both to select which label formats appear in the list of available labels.

6. In the Labels list, click on or scroll to the label format you want, or type the first few letters of the label type. When you highlight a label, the Label Details area and the sample labels in the dialog box will reflect your current selection. (If the label format you need isn't available, create it yourself, as described below.)

7. When you find the format you want, double-click the format or highlight it and choose Select.

To Type Text for Labels

1. Select a label format as described above.

2. Type each line in the label, pressing ↵ between lines.

3. To start the next label, press Ctrl+↵.

4. Repeat steps 2 and 3 as needed.

To Create, Edit, or Delete a Label Format

1. Optionally, choose File ➤ Print ➤ Select to select the printer you'll be using to print the labels. Return to the document window.

2.   Optionally, place the cursor where you want the new label size to take effect.

3.   Choose For_mat ➤ La_bels. The Labels dialog box opens.

4.   Choose one of the options below:

- To *create* a new label format, choose _Create.

- To *edit* a label format, highlight it in the _Labels list and choose _Edit.

- To *delete* a label format, highlight it in the _Labels list and choose _Delete, then choose _Yes. Skip to step 6.

5.   Fill in the Create Labels or Edit Labels dialog box (see Options, below). Choose OK when done.

6.   Choose Cancel to exit the dialog box without selecting a label format, or highlight the format you want and choose _Select to select a label format.

OPTIONS   These options are available in the Create Labels (or Edit Labels) dialog box. As you make changes, the sample label page at the lower-right corner of the dialog box will reflect your latest choices.

Label Description   A unique description for the label.

Label Type   Determines which list or lists will display your new format in the Labels dialog box. (Choose La_ser, Tractor-Fe_d, or _Both.)

Change   Lets you select a paper size.

Label Size   Lets you specify the _Width and Height of a single label.

Labels Per Page   Lets you specify the number of _Columns and _Rows in each sheet of labels.

Top Left Label   Lets you define the location of the first label. Specify the _Top Edge and L_eft Edge.

Distance Between Labels   Lets you define the distance between labels. For Col_umns, type the distance between columns (the physical space between adjacent labels). For R_ows, type the distance between two rows.

Label Margins   Lets you specify the Left, Right, Top, and Bottom margins for a single label.

 NOTES   You can merge information from a merge data file onto labels. Simply select a mailing label format at the top of the form file and perform the merge as usual. (See the Merge Operations entry.)

SEE ALSO   *Envelope, Merge Operations, Paper Size*

LANGUAGE

The Language feature allows you to choose among optional foreign language modules that offer various language-dependent features, and to enable or disable the writing tools in all or part of your document.

To Choose a Different Language

1.   Move the cursor where the new setting should take effect, or select a block of text.

2.   Choose Tools ➤ Language.

3.   Select the language from the displayed Current Language list, or type the first few letters of the language name. (The language module must already be installed on your computer.)

4.   Choose OK.

To Disable or Enable the Writing Tools

1.   Repeat steps 1 and 2 of the previous procedure.

2. To disable the tools, select (check) Disable Writing Tools (In This Portion Of The Text). To enable the tools, deselect the option.

3. Choose OK.

NOTES The currently selected language determines which Spell Checker, Thesaurus, Grammatik, and Hyphenation files Word-Perfect will use; the sort order for Sort features; and the language used to display date text and "(continued...)" messages in footnotes.

You can control text for certain features (such as month names) in various languages by editing the WP.LRS language resource file.

SEE ALSO *Grammatik, Hyphenation, Inital Codes Style, Spell Checker, Thesaurus*

LINE HEIGHT

Line height is the distance between the baseline of one line and the baseline of the next.

To Set Line Height

1. Move the cursor where the new setting should take effect, or select a block of text.

2. Choose Format ➤ Line ➤ Height.

3. Choose either Auto or Fixed.

4. If you chose Fixed, press Tab and enter a line height measurement.

5. Choose OK.

NOTES   If you choose Auto (the default), WordPerfect adds 2 points of space to proportionally spaced fonts and automatically adjusts line height to match the space required for the largest font on a line.

If you choose Fixed, lines will have the height you specify and be evenly spaced, regardless of the font size. Fixed line heights are often used with baseline placement for typesetting (see the Typesetting entry).

Setting the line height has no effect on printers that can print only six lines per inch.

To specify the amount of white space that appears between paragraphs, choose Format ➤ Paragraph ➤ Format ➤ Spacing Between Paragraphs (see the Paragraph entry).

SEE ALSO   *Font, Initial Codes Style, Line Spacing, Paragraph, Typesetting*

LINE NUMBERING

WordPerfect lets you display and print line numbers on a document. You can change the numbering scheme and position of the number on the line. (Line numbers are not visible in Draft view.)

To Turn Line Numbering On or Off

1. Move the cursor to where the new setting should take effect, or select a block of text.

2. Choose Format ➤ Line ➤ Numbering.

3. To turn line numbering on, select (check) Turn Line Numbering On and continue with step 4. To turn line numbering off, deselect the option and continue with step 5.

4. Adjust the line numbering options, position, and other aspects of the line number appearance if you wish (see Options, below).

5. Choose OK.

OPTIONS The line numbering options are as follows:

Font Lets you choose the font for line numbers. Make your selections and choose OK.

Numbering Method Lets you choose a numbering method for line numbers. Your options are Number (default), Lowercase Letter, Uppercase Letter, Lowercase Roman, and Uppercase Roman.

Starting Line Number Sets the starting number for line numbering (usually 1).

First Printing Line Number Sets the first line number actually printed (usually 1).

Numbering Interval Numbers only every *n*th line; enter a number (e.g., *5* will number every fifth line).

From Left Edge Of Page Moves line numbers a specified distance from the left edge of the paper or from the center of the space between columns. Select this option, press Tab, then enter a measurement. This option is the default.

Left Of Margin Moves line numbers left by a specified distance from the left margin. Select this option, press Tab, then enter a measurement.

Restart Numbering On Each Page When selected, starts line numbers with 1 at the beginning of a new page. When deselected, lines are numbered continuously through the document.

Number All Newspaper Columns When selected (checked), WordPerfect numbers lines in newspaper columns. Left Of Margin is selected automatically and the position setting is reduced.

Count Blank Lines Select (check) this option to count blank lines. Deselect this option to prevent WordPerfect from numbering or counting blank lines.

NOTES   Headers, footers, and blank lines created by your choices for line spacing are not counted in line numbers.

To add a vertical separator line between the line numbers and the text, choose Graphics ➤ Vertical Line (or press Ctrl+Shift+F11).

SEE ALSO   *Font; Graphic Lines; Headers, Footers, and Watermarks; Initial Codes Style*

LINE SPACING

Line spacing determines the number of lines that will be inserted after each soft return [SRt] or hard return [HRt] code. Single spacing is the default.

To Set Line Spacing

1.   Move the cursor to where the new setting should take effect, or select a block of text.

2.   Choose Format ➤ Line ➤ Spacing.

3.   Enter the line spacing you want (in whole numbers or fractions) and choose OK.

NOTES   The value you set for line spacing is multiplied by the line height to determine the actual distance between lines (e.g., if line spacing is 2.5 and line height is 0.5", lines will be printed 1.25" apart, baseline to baseline).

You can also use the Line Spacing button on the power bar to change line spacing.

 **SEE ALSO** *Initial Codes Style, Line Height, Make It Fit Expert, Power Bar, Typesetting*

LIST

The List feature generates automatic lists of tables, figures, maps, illustrations, or anything else you want. This involves three steps:

1. Mark items (see below) and assign them to a list. You don't need to mark captions for graphic boxes.

2. Define the list's location, appearance, and whether it contains graphic box captions.

3. Generate the lists.

List features are available when the List feature bar is visible.

To Display or Close the List Feature Bar

• To display the feature bar, choose Tools ➤ List

• To hide the feature bar, choose the Close button in the feature bar.

To Mark a List Item

1. Display the List feature bar.

2. Select the text, including any codes that should appear in the list.

3. Click the List drop-down button and type in (or edit) a list name, or choose a list name for the selected text.

4. Choose Mark.

Repeat steps 2– 4 for each item you want to mark.

To Define a List

1. Move the cursor to the location where you want the list to appear.

2. Display the List feature bar.

3. Click the Define button in the feature bar.

4. If necessary, create a new list or retrieve lists from an existing file.

- To create a new list, click Create and type a unique name for the list. Optionally, select items from Numbering Format, Current Style, and Auto Reference Box Captions to change the numbering format for page numbers, the list style, and referencing of graphics box captions. Choose OK. (See Options, below.)

- To retrieve a list from a file, click Retrieve. In the Filename text box, type the file name that contains the lists you want, or use the file button to locate the file. Choose OK. Select (check) the lists you want to retrieve and choose OK again.

5. Highlight the list you want to insert into the document and choose Insert or press ↵ (or double-click the list name).

Be sure to define and insert separate lists for each type of graphics box caption you want to track.

To Generate a List

1. Display the List feature bar.
2. Click the <u>G</u>enerate button in the feature bar.
3. Choose OK.

OPTIONS You can use these options in the Create List (or Edit List) dialog box to control the appearance of list entries.

Position Lets you define where the page number appears with respect to the text of the index entry.

Page Numbering Lets you define the format of the page number.

Change Lets you change the style of the list entries.

Auto Reference Box Captions Lets you automatically create a list of graphics box captions for a specified type of graphics box.

NOTES You can create lists for an individual document or for a master document. Place the list definition in the master document, *not* in a subdocument.

Generated list items will be in the order in which they appear in the document.

To delete a list item, turn on Reveal Codes (Alt+F3) and delete the appropriate [Mrk Txt List] code. Then regenerate the list.

SEE ALSO *Cross-Reference, Generate, Graphics and Graphics Boxes, Index, Master Document, Page Numbering, Table of Authorities, Table of Contents*

MACROS

Macros let you record the sequences of keystrokes and mouse selections that perform a certain task. You can then "play back" (run or execute) those commands later.

The WordPerfect macro language is a full-featured programming language that lets you write complex macros and interact with the user. You can use the Macro tools toolbar to access most macro features quickly.

The macro features have changed between versions 6.0 and 6.1. Most importantly, the options for working with macros stored in a disk file (.wcm) and macros stored in a template file (.wpt) are now separate: use Tools ➤ Macro for disk macros and Tools ➤ Template Macro for template macros. Other changes: the Macros button bar is now the Macro Tools toolbar; the Macro Edit feature bar was redesigned; and you can no longer use the Macros dialog boxes to add macros to menus (use the Menu Bar Preferences options instead; see *Preferences*).

To Display the Macro Tools Toolbar

1. If no toolbar is visible, choose View ➤ Toolbar.

2. Right-click the toolbar and choose Macro Tools from the QuickMenu.

To Record a Macro

1. Do whatever it takes to set the stage for your macro. For example, if the macro will italicize selected text, type in and select some text.

2. *For disk macros*, choose Tools ➤ Macro ➤ Record (or press Ctrl+F10, or click the Record button in the Macro Tools toolbar). *For template macros*, choose Tools ➤ Template Macro ➤ Record.

3. Optionally, if you are recording a template macro, click the Location button in the Record Template Macro dialog box and select a location for the macro (see *Options,* below), then choose OK.

4. Choose a name for your macro:

  • For macros stored in a template, type a unique name.

  • For macros stored on disk, type a valid DOS file name (one to eight characters, no spaces, punctuation, or extension). Or, to create a Ctrl+Shift+*key* macro, press Ctrl and Shift, plus a letter (for example, press Ctrl+Shift+A).

5. Choose Record.

6. If the macro already exists, you'll be asked if you want to replace it. Choose Yes (to overwrite) or No to return to the document window.

7. The Macro Edit feature bar appears, and the message "Macro Record" appears in the status bar. Type the keystrokes you want to record, including any menu choices and shortcuts. (See *Notes,* below.)

8. To stop recording and save a *disk macro,* do one of the following: choose Tools ➤ Macro ➤ Record; press Ctrl+F10, click the Record button in the Macro Tools toolbar; or click the Stop Macro Play Or Record button in the Macro Edit feature bar. To stop recording and save a *template macro,* choose Tools ➤ Template Macro ➤ Record or click the Stop Macro Play Or Record button in the Macro Edit feature bar.

To Play a Macro

1. Move the cursor to where you want the macro to start, or select the text it will act on.

2. If the macro is a Ctrl+Shift+*key* disk macro, press the Ctrl+Shift+*key* combination (for example, Ctrl+Shift+A). The macro will run, and you can skip steps 3–6 below.

3. *For disk macros*, choose Tools ➤ Macro ➤ Play, press
    Alt+F10, or click the Play button in the Macro Tools
    toolbar. *For template macros*, choose Tools ➤ Template
    Macro ➤ Play.

4. Optionally, if you are playing a template macro, click the
    Location button in the Play Template Macro dialog box
    and select a location for the macro, and then choose OK.

5. Type in or highlight the macro name.

6. Choose Play. The macro will play back your recorded
    keystrokes.

To Edit a Macro

Macros are stored in standard WordPerfect documents. This makes
hem easy to edit, format, and print.

1. *For disk macros*, choose Tools ➤ Macro ➤ Edit, or click the
    Edit Macro button in the Macro Tools toolbar. *For template
    macros*, choose Tools ➤ Template Macro ➤ Edit.

2. Optionally, if you are editing a template macro, click the
    Location button in the Edit Template Macro dialog box
    and select a location for the macro, then choose OK.

3. Type in or highlight the macro name.

4. Choose Edit. Your macro, and the Macro Edit feature bar,
    will appear.

5. Edit your macro using normal text editing techniques. Be
    sure to use proper macro programming language com-
    mands. Here are some special techniques you can use
    while editing a macro:

    • To insert recorded macro commands at the cursor posi-
       tion, click the Begin Recording To The Current Document
       button in the feature bar. Record your keystrokes and
       menu selections normally. When you're done, click the
       Stop Macro Play Or Record button in the feature bar.

- To create and manage macro dialog boxes, click the Dialog Editor button in the feature bar. (This button is for serious macro programmers! Click the Help button in the Macro Dialogs dialog box for more information.)

- To insert programming commands at the cursor position, click the Commands button in the feature bar. Use the Type button and the list boxes to select your command, edit the command if necessary, and choose Insert. When you're finished, choose Close.

- To insert a code at the cursor position, click the Codes button in the feature bar, and then double-click the code you want. When you're finished, choose Close.

6. When you're done making changes, compile and save your macro as explained next.

To Save and Compile a Macro

Whenever you create or edit a macro, WordPerfect *compiles* it once before running it. During compiling, WordPerfect checks for errors and puts the macro into code the computer can understand. Once you're done editing a macro, use any of the following methods to save and compile it.

- To *save, compile and close* the macro editing window, choose Options ➤ Close Macro in the Macro Edit feature bar, then choose Yes if prompted to save changes. WordPerfect will compile the macro if necessary and close the macro editing window and feature bar.

- To *save, compile, and stay* in the macro editing window, click Save & Compile in the feature bar.

- To *save and compile changes in a new disk or template macro,* click Options, then choose Save As Macro (to save a disk macro) or Save As Template Macro (to save a template macro). Optionally, if you are saving a template macro, click the Location button in the Template Macro Save As dialog box and select a location for the macro, then choose OK. Specify a name for your macro and choose Save. You'll remain in the macro editing window, but the new version of the macro you are editing will appear on screen.

OPTIONS The dialog boxes for managing template macros have Delete and Location buttons, and all dialog boxes for managing macros have a Help button.

Delete Lets you delete a macro from a template. Specify the macro you want to delete and click Delete.

Location Lets you choose the location of a macro. Your options are Current Template (the template for the current document file); Default Template (the default template specified in File Preferences); Use As Default (uses the selected location as the default for future template macro operations).

Help Provides helpful information about using the macro dialog boxes.

NOTES To play a recently-used macro, choose Tools ➤ Macro or Tools ➤ Template Macro and select the macro name. To assign *any* macro to a menu bar that you have created, see *Preferences*.)

To play a macro assigned to a button on the toolbar, click the button. (See *Preferences*.)

To play a macro assigned to a certain keystroke combination on the keyboard, press that combination. (See *Preferences*.)

To stop a running macro, press Esc (or click the Play button on the Macro Tools toolbar) and OK to remove the macro canceled message from your screen. Then review the document and fix any unwanted changes that the macro made.

While recording a macro, you can insert a *PauseKey (Key: Enter!)* command that makes the macro wait for the user to type something and press ↵ during playback. To insert this command, click the Pause While Recording/Executing A Macro button in the feature bar. Click the button again to continue recording the macro.

While recording a macro, you can have WordPerfect pause at a dialog box when the macro is played back. Simply open the dialog box the normal way, then select (check) Show Dialog at the upper-right corner and choose OK.

For information about macro programming, choose Help ➤ Macros from the WordPerfect menu bar.

Macros stored on disk have the extension .WCM. Macros stored in disk files can be run from *any* WordPerfect document. Macros stored in templates can be run only from documents that use those templates. You can, however, copy macros from one template to another. (See *Template.*) You can also save disk macros as template macros, and vice-versa.

Ctrl+Shift+*key* macros offer the quickest way to run a macro. They're stored on disk with names like CTRLSFTA.WCM (for the macro named by pressing Ctrl+Shift+A).

If you record keystrokes in error, you can record the macro again or edit the macro.

When recording a macro, you can use your mouse or keyboard to record any text you type, most editing and cursor movement keys (like ↵, ↓, ↑, and Backspace), commands you choose, and responses to dialog boxes.

To select text, you must use keyboard techniques such as Shift+arrow or Edit ➤ Select. (See *Selecting Text.*)

 SEE ALSO   *Preferences, Selecting Text, Template, Toolbar*

MAIL

If your network has Windows mail software that's compatible with WordPerfect, you can use network mail directly from WordPerfect.

See your network administrator for details about what features your network mail program offers.

To Access Network Mail from WordPerfect

1. Sign on to your network.

2. Start Windows and WordPerfect for Windows.

3. Open the document you want to send as a mail message. You can select a portion of the document if you wish.

4. Choose File ➤ Send. If a submenu appears, choose the mail system you want to use.

5. If necessary, enter your mail user name and password.

6. Use your mail system as required to send, read, and respond to messages.

7. When you're ready to return to WordPerfect, choose an appropriate "close" or "exit" command.

 **SEE ALSO** *Install*

The Make It Fit Expert can expand or shrink your document to fill a specified number of pages. It does this by adjusting margins, font size, and line spacing as needed.

To Make Your Document Fit

1. Open the document that you want to adjust.

2. Choose Format ➤ Make It Fit Expert, or click the Make It Fit button in the WordPerfect toolbar.

3. Enter the Desired Number Of Filled Pages you want in the final document.

4. Select (check) the items you want to adjust automatically. Deselect (clear) items that should not be adjusted. Your options are Left Margin, Right Margin, Top Margin, Bottom Margin, Font Size, and Line Spacing.

5. Choose Make It Fit.

NOTES Be reasonable when specifying the number of pages the Make It Fit Expert should create. Requesting too many or too few pages may lead to ugly documents.

If you don't like the Make It Fit results, immediately choose Edit ➤ Undo, press Ctrl+Z, or click the Undo button in the toolbar.

SEE ALSO Font, Line Spacing, Margins

MARGINS

A margin is the white space between the text and the edge of a printed page. The default margin settings are 1 inch.

To Set Margins

1. Position the cursor where you want the margin changes to start, or select one or more paragraphs of text to limit the changes to those paragraphs.

2. Choose Format ➤ Margins, press Ctrl+F8, or double-click the top portion of the ruler bar.

3. Enter the measurements for the Left, Right, Top, or Bottom margin.

4. Choose OK.

You can also use the ruler bar to set the left or right margin:

1. Repeat step 1 above.

2. If the ruler isn't visible, choose View ➤ Ruler Bar or press Alt+Shift+F3.

3. Drag the left or right margin marker near the top of the ruler to the margin position you want. As you drag, a dotted vertical line appears and moves to show the changing

margin, and the status bar will indicate the current position of the margin.

NOTES   To temporarily change the left margin or the left and right margins for the current paragraph, use Indent (F7) or Double Indent (Ctrl+Shift+F7). To temporarily move the left margin back by one tab stop, press Shift+Tab, or choose Format ➤ Paragraph ➤ Back Tab. (See the Indent entry.)

To adjust margins for future paragraphs or selected paragraphs, use Format ➤ Paragraph ➤ Format. (See *Paragraph.*)

SEE ALSO   *Binding, Indent, Initial Codes Style, Make It Fit Expert, Paragraph, Ruler, Tabs, Typesetting, Units of Measure*

MASTER DOCUMENT

Master documents let you create large documents from smaller, more manageable subdocuments. You can also combine the subdocuments to create indexes, tables of contents, lists, and other addenda for the master document.

To Link a
Subdocument to a Master Document

1.   Move the cursor to the place in the master document where you want to link the subdocument.

2.   Optionally, press Ctrl+↵ to start the subdocument on a new page.

3.   Choose File ➤ Master Document ➤ Subdocument.

4.   Enter or highlight the subdocument file name. The subdocument need not exist when you create the link.

5. Click Include. A [Subdoc] code appears at the location of the subdocument link.

To Expand a Master Document

Expanding a master document retrieves the existing linked sub-documents into their respective link locations.

1. Choose File ➤ Master Document ➤ Expand Master.

2. Select (check) the subdocuments you want to expand. (You can use the Mark button to Mark All or Clear All check boxes at once.)

3. Choose OK.

To Condense a Master Document

Condensing a master document removes the linked subdocument text but retains the links:

1. Choose File ➤ Master Document ➤ Condense Master.

2. Select (check) the subdocuments you want to condense and the ones you want to save. You only need to save sub-documents that you changed while editing the master document. (You can use the Mark button to Condense All, Clear Condense, Save All, or Clear Save.)

3. Choose OK.

To Structure
Master Documents and Subdocuments

The master document should be a skeleton structure for your final document. It should contain only the following:

- Formatting codes that apply to *all* subdocuments

- Links to each subdocument

- Titles and definitions for endnote location, tables of authorities, tables of contents, indexes, and lists

Subdocuments should contain everything else needed to build the final document, including:

- Text and graphics for each chapter, section, etc.

- Formatting codes specific to each subdocument

- Marked text for cross-references, footnotes, endnotes, tables of authorities, tables of contents, indexes, and lists

To Generate Lists for Master Documents

You can choose whether to save changes to subdocuments when you generate lists for a master document.

1. Choose Tools ➤ Generate or press Ctrl+F9, then choose Options.

2. Select (check) Save Subdocuments to save the changes; deselect the option to generate the lists without saving changes first (this will be faster).

3. Choose OK twice to start generating the lists.

NOTES Typically, you'll edit the subdocuments separately, then use a master document to assemble them, but you can also edit the text of an expanded master document, including subdocument text.

In draft view, subdocument links appear as comments containing *Subdoc:* followed by the path name of the subdocument. In Page view or Two-Page view, subdocuments appear as icons that you can click to see the subdocument name. In Reveal Codes (Alt+F3), the linked subdocuments are marked by [Subdoc] or [Subdoc Begin] and [Subdoc End] codes.

You must expand a master document before printing, unless you actually want to print the condensed version.

You don't have to expand a master document before generating lists, tables of contents, and similar items.

SEE ALSO *Comment, Cross-Reference, Footnotes and End-notes, Generate, Index, List, Table of Authorities, Table of Contents*

MENUS

WordPerfect for Windows uses the standard Windows Common User Access (CUA) conventions—pull-down menus, dialog boxes, buttons, and scroll bars—to provide access to its features. This entry discusses the use of pull-down menus and of the available keystroke alternatives to the various elements of the CUA.

To Choose Menu Options

To use the mouse to choose a menu option:

1. Click on the menu name.

2. Move the mouse pointer to the desired option.

3. Click on the option.

4. Repeat steps 2 and 3 as needed to move through any submenus.

To use the keyboard to select a menu option:

- Press the Alt key and press the underlined letter of the menu you want. Then press the underlined letter of the option you want.

Here's another way to select a menu option using the keyboard:

1. Press, then release the Alt key to activate the menu bar.

2. Use the arrow keys to highlight the menu you want to open and press ⌐, ↓, or ↑ to reveal the menu. Press ↑ or ↓ to move *within* a menu. Press ← or → to move *across* the menu bar or to open additional submenus.

3. Press ⌐ when the option you want is highlighted.

To Cancel a Menu Choice

- Click the menu name or any empty space outside the menu.

- Press and release Alt, F10, or Esc.

To Use Shortcut Keystrokes

Hold down the first key while pressing the second key. For example, to press Shift+F4, hold down Shift, press F4, and then release both keys.

NOTES Table III describes some of the symbols used on pull-down menus.

You can set up custom menus of your own, or edit existing menus if they were not predefined by WordPerfect. Choose Edit ➤ Preferences and double-click Menu Bar, or right-click the menu bar and choose Preferences.

Table III: WordPerfect Menu Symbols

SYMBOL	MEANING
... (ellipsis)	Choosing the menu option will take you to a dialog box
Dimmed (grayed)	A dimmed option is currenly unavailable
Check Mark (✔)	The checked option is currently active ("on")
Triangle (➤)	Leads to another submenu of additional commands
shortcut key	Indicates a shortcut key (such as F4) or a keystroke comination (such as Shift+F4) that you can use instead of choosing menu options

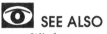 **SEE ALSO**   *Cancel, Dialog Boxes, Help, Hide Bars, Preferences, Windows*

MERGE OPERATIONS

Merge operations combine information from two sources into a single document. For example, you can use merging to print form letters addressed to many different people.

Merging involves three basic operations:

- Creating a data file of variable information (e.g., names and addresses)

- Creating a form file of standard information (e.g., a form letter)

- Merging the two files into a new document. The merge data can also come from the keyboard or a text file.

To Create a Data File

1.   Choose Tools ➤ Merge, or press Shift+F9.

2.   If you want to place the records in a WordPerfect table, select (check) Place Records In A Table.

3.   Click the Data button.

4.   If there's already information in the current document, you'll be asked if you want to use the current document or open a new one. Select an option and choose OK. The Create Data File dialog box appears.

5.   For each *field* you want to define (see Notes, below), enter a field name (up to 40 characters, including spaces), then choose Add or press ↵.

   - Add field names in the same order that data will be entered.

- If you need to rearrange fields or change field names, click a name in the field list and use the Replace, Delete, Move Up, or Move Down buttons to change the field name or position.

6. When you're done entering field names, choose OK. The Quick Data Entry dialog box will appear.

7. For each field in a *record* (see Notes, below), type the data and press ↵ or click Next Field. When you finish typing the last field in a record, pressing ↵ will automatically start the next record.

8. If necessary, use the buttons in the Quick Data Entry dialog box to move from field to field, add new records, delete records, find records, or edit the field names. When you're done adding data, choose Close.

9. You'll be asked if you want to save your changes. To save your changes now, choose Yes, enter a file name, and choose OK. To skip the save for now, choose No.

10. The Merge feature bar will appear. You can use its buttons to make further changes if you wish (see Options, below).

11. When you're done, choose File ➤ Close, and save your changes if prompted.

To Create a Form File

1. Choose Tools ➤ Merge, or press Shift+F9.

2. Choose Form.

3. If there's already information in the current document, you'll be asked if you want to use the current document or open a new one. Select an option and choose OK.

4. If you want to associate a data file with this form file, select Associate A Data File, and type the data file name and extension (or use the file button to locate the file). If you don't want to associate a data file, choose None. Then choose OK. The Merge feature bar will appear.

5. Place any formatting options you want for the merged document in the Initial Codes Style.

6. Type your form file (e.g., type a letter) until you come to a place where you want to insert a field from a data file, a date code, a merge code, or a prompt for data entry from the keyboard.

7. Choose an appropriate button from the Merge feature bar (see Options, below) and fill in any dialog boxes that appear.

8. Repeat steps 6 and 7 until you're done typing the form.

9. Save your changes and close the file (File ➤ Close ➤ Yes).

To Edit a Data or Form File

To edit a data or form file that you've already saved and closed,

1. Open it as you would any normal file (choose File ➤ Open, Ctrl+O, or the Open button on the toolbar).

2. Use normal editing techniques and the buttons on the Merge feature bar to make your changes (see Options, below). Be careful not to delete any merge commands or page breaks unless you know what they're for.

3. Save your changes and close the file (File ➤ Close ➤ Yes).

To Perform a Merge

1. Choose Tools ➤ Merge, or press Shift+F9.

2. Choose Merge. The Perform Merge dialog box opens.

3. In the Form File text box, specify the form file or use the button in the text box to select a file on disk, the current document, or the Clipboard.

4. In the Data File text box, specify the data file. You can use the button in the text box to select a file on disk, no document (if all the input is from the keyboard), or the Clipboard.

5. In the Output File text box, specify the output file. You can use the button in the text box to select the current document, new document, printer, or a file on disk.

6. Optionally, choose buttons described below. Fill in the dialog boxes that appear and choose OK until you return to the Perform Merge dialog box.

Select Records Lets you choose which records are included in the merge. You can either specify the conditions for included records (based on field value or record number range) or mark records individually.

Envelopes Lets you format an envelope for each record in the output file.

Options Lets you customize the format of the output file and choose options for keyboard merges.

Reset Returns the Select Records, Envelopes, and Options settings to their previous values.

7. When you're ready to perform the merge, choose OK.

8. If the data file is not a WordPerfect file, the Convert File Format dialog box will open. Select the format you want to convert from and choose OK. For example, you would choose *ANSI Delimited Text (Windows)* for a Microsoft Excel spreadsheet that you saved in "Text" format.

To Change Default Settings for Delimited Text Files

The data file can contain delimited text format data, such as that exported from spreadsheet and database files. The default field delimiter for a comma separated value (comma delimited) text file is a comma. The record delimiter is a carriage return–linefeed sequence [CR][LF]. Strings of characters are enclosed in double-quotation marks ("). To change the default settings:

• Choose Edit ➤ Preferences, double-click Convert, change the settings as needed, and choose OK, then Close.

To Interact with a Merge

When defining a form file, you can use the K̲eyboard button in the Merge feature bar to request input from the user. During the merge, WordPerfect will pause at the KEYBOARD command, display the message you entered as a prompt, and wait for keyboard input. Respond by typing the required data, then choose C̲ontinue from the feature bar to continue the merge.

Choose these options from the feature bar during a keyboard merge.

Continue To continue the merge.

Skip Record To skip the current record and go on to the next. Click continue after choosing this button.

Quit To stop the merge after including any remaining text.

Stop To stop the merge at the cursor position.

OPTIONS Choose any of these buttons on the Merge feature bar when you create or change a *data file*:

Row (Table data files only.) Lets you insert or delete a row (record) in the table.

Column (Table data files only.) Lets you insert or delete a column (field name) in the table.

End Field (Non-table data files only.) Ends the data field at the cursor position. You can also press Alt+↵ to end a field.

End Record (Non-table data files only.) Ends the data record at the cursor position. You can also press Alt+Shift+↵ to end a record.

Merge Codes Lets you insert merge codes (commands) from the Insert Merge Codes list. To select a code, highlight it in the Insert Merge Codes dialog box and choose I̲nsert, or double-click the code. To highlight a code quickly, type the first few letters of its name.

Quick Entry Goes to the Quick Data Entry dialog box, which makes it easy to enter records. See "To Create a Data File" (steps 7–10) above for details.

Merge Opens the Merge dialog box. (Same as choosing T̲ools ➤ Merge or pressing Alt+F9.)

Go To Form Lets you switch to a form file. If no form file is currently associated with the data file, you'll be asked to select or create one.

Options Lets you sort or print the data file, control the appearance of merge codes, and remove the Merge feature bar.

Choose any of these buttons on the Merge feature bar when you create or change a *form file:*

Insert Field Inserts a field name and code at the cursor position. Choose Insert Field to open the Insert Field Name Or Number dialog box. You can double-click a field name in the Field Names list (or highlight it and choose Insert). If the Field Names list is empty, or you want to insert fields from a different data file, choose Data File, select the file you want, and choose OK.

Date Inserts a DATE code at the cursor position. During a merge, this code will be replaced by the system date.

Merge Codes Same as the Merge Codes button for data files, described above.

Keyboard Inserts a KEYBOARD code at the cursor position. Choose Keyboard, enter the prompt you want to display during a merge, and choose OK. During a merge, WordPerfect will pause at the KEYBOARD code and let the user enter data.

Merge Same as Merge button for data files, described above.

Go To Data Lets you switch to a data file. If no data file is currently associated with the form file, you'll be asked to select or create one.

Options Lets you control the appearance of merge codes and remove the Merge feature bar.

NOTES Each complete piece of information in the data file is called a *record,* and each record is divided into one or more *fields.* For example, a customer record might include the fields *Last Name, First Name, Middle Initial, Street Address, City, State, Zip Code,* and so on.

The *data file* contains the data to be inserted into the form file. Data files can contain many records separated by merge codes or arranged in a table. It's usually easier to enter data if you store it as a table.

If you omit the extension when typing a data file name, Word-Perfect will use the extension .DAT.

Table data files can have up to 64 columns (fields). Non-tabular data files can have up to 255 fields.

Data files also can come from the keyboard or a delimited text file. (Many database, spreadsheet, and word processing programs can create delimited text files.)

Before merging, you can sort the data file or select records from it. (See *Options* (above) and *Sorting and Selecting*.)

A *form file* contains standard text, graphics, and formatting information; field names indicating where to insert data from the data file; and, optionally, other merge commands.

If you omit the extension when typing a form file name, WordPerfect will use the extension. FRM.

The form file can insert and reuse fields from the data file in any order. It need not use every field in the data file.

During a merge, information from the data file, keyboard, or delimited text file is substituted into the appropriate fields of the form file, and the file is formatted automatically.

⊚ SEE ALSO *Envelope, Find, Initial Codes Style, Preferences, Sorting and Selecting, Tables*

MOUSE

The mouse makes it easy to navigate the WordPerfect for Windows graphical user interface. Most mouse operations in WordPerfect are the same ones used in other Windows applications.

To Use Your Mouse

Here are some commonly-used mouse terms:

Click Press the left button and release immediately.

Double-click Click the left button two times quickly.

Drag Press the left button and hold it down while moving the mouse. Release the mouse button when you're done.

Right-click Click the right button.

To Select Text

To select text for cutting and pasting, changing fonts, or other operations:

1. Position the cursor at the start of the text.

2. Press and hold down the left mouse button.

3. Drag the mouse pointer to the end of the text. The text the mouse pointer passes over will be highlighted.

4. Release the mouse button.

To deselect the text, click the left mouse button again.

To select a word, double-click it. To select a sentence, triple-click it. To select a paragraph, quadruple-click it. Or move the pointer to the left margin (the pointer changes to an arrow) and click once to select a sentence or twice to select a paragraph. Or, move the pointer to the left margin, right-click, and choose "Select …" options from the QuickMenu.

You can extend your selection of a word, sentence, or paragraph "chunk" to the next or previous chunk of the same size by holding down the Shift key and clicking (or dragging to) the next or previous chunk. You can repeat this "QuickSelect" (Shift+click or Shift+drag) action until you've selected all the text you want.

To select a rectangular chunk of text, hold down the Shift key while dragging with the *right* mouse button.

To select columns that are separated by tabs or indents, hold down the Ctrl key while dragging with the *right* mouse button.

To Choose Menu and Dialog Box Options

- To choose menu options, click on the menu name, then click on the item you want. Or click on the menu name, drag the mouse to the item you want, then release the button.

- To select an item from a list box and take the default action, double-click the item. Or click the item and choose the default button (the one with the dark outline).

- To turn a check box item on or off, move the mouse pointer to the check box and click the mouse button.

- To select a radio button, click it.

To Use Graphics Boxes

- To select a graphics box, click anywhere in the box. To de-select it, click outside the box.

- To move a graphics box, select the box and drag it to the new location. The mouse pointer appears as a four-headed arrow when you can move the box.

- To size a box, select the box, then drag one of the square handles along the box border to achieve the desired size. The mouse appears as a two-headed arrow when you can size the box.

- To open the editor for the graphics box, double-click anywhere in the box.

To Open a QuickMenu

- Right-click a "hot spot" on the screen. Then click the left or right mouse button on the option you want. (See the QuickMenu entry.)

To Open a Dialog Box from Reveal Codes

- Turn on Reveal Codes (Alt+F3) and double-click the code for the feature you want to change. The dialog box for that feature will open. (This works for many codes.)

NOTES   Before using the mouse, you must install it as explained in your documentation and then set up the mouse for use with Windows. Customize your mouse's behavior through the Windows Control Panel.

Always click the left mouse button, unless otherwise directed (or unless you have switched the left and right button functions).

Whenever you move the mouse pointer to a button in the toolbar, power bar, feature bar, status bar, or graphics toolbar, WordPerfect will display a short message in the title bar about what that button does. If you've elected to display the toolbar or power bar buttons as pictures, a QuickTip will appear near the pointer when you move the mouse pointer to a button. (You can turn off the Help prompts and QuickTips in Preferences, though there's no good reason to do so.)

SEE ALSO   *Dialog Boxes, Graphics and Graphics Boxes, Menus, QuickMenu, Preferences, Reveal Codes, Selecting Text*

NEW

You can open a new blank document window at any time (up to a limit of nine documents).

To Open a New Document Window

- Press Ctrl+N, Shift+F4, or click the New Blank Document button in the toolbar.

To Open a New Document Window with Any Template

1. Choose File ➤ New, press Ctrl+T, or click the New Document button in the WordPerfect toolbar.

2. In the Group list, click the group that contains the template you want.

3. In the Select Template list, highlight the description for the template you want and choose Select (or just double-click the template description).

4. Respond to any prompts that appear.

You also can edit and create templates if you wish. (See *Template*.)

👁 **SEE ALSO** *Open, Preferences, Save/Save As, Template*

OBJECT LINKING AND EMBEDDING

You can use object linking and embedding (OLE) to link or embed graphics images, text, charts, spreadsheets, sound clips, video clips, and other Windows objects in a WordPerfect document or another application. For linked objects, if the source object changes in WordPerfect or the application that created the object, the object will be updated automatically in both places. OLE 2 support is new in wordPefect 6.1. (See your Windows documentation for more details on OLE.)

WordPerfect offers several ways to link or embed objects:

- Insert ➤ Object (described below)

- Edit ➤ Paste Special ➤ Paste Link (described below)

- Insert ➤ Spreadsheet/Database (see *Spreadsheet/Database Import and Link*).

- Graphics menu options, including Image, Draw, Chart, and Text Art (see the related entries).

To Embed an Object

1. Choose Insert ➤ Object ➤ Create New.

2. Highlight the Object Type you want and choose OK (or double-click your choice). The server application for the object will open.

3. Create the object (Paintbrush picture, spreadsheet, etc.).

4. When you're done creating the object, do one of the steps below. The embedded object will appear in a graphics box in your document.

   • If you are editing in-place (within the WordPerfect document window), click in the WordPerfect document window, outside the object.

   • If you are editing in a separate application window, choose File ➤ Exit & Return To... (or whatever commands normally exit the application). If you are prompted to save your changes, choose Yes.

5. If necessary, deselect the object by clicking outside the object again.

To Link an Entire Saved Object

1. Choose Insert ➤ Object ➤ Create From File.

2. In the File text box, type the file name of the object to be linked, or use the file button to locate the file and fill in the File box.

3. Select (check) Link.

4. Choose OK.

To Paste Link an Object

1. While WordPerfect is running, switch to Program Manager (Ctrl+Esc or Alt+Tab).

2. Open the server application for the object you want to paste link into your WordPerfect document.

3. In the server application, create and save the file you want to paste link, or open an existing file.The server file must be saved.

4. Select the object or portion of the object you want to link, then cut or copy the selection to the Clipboard.

5. Switch back to WordPerfect (Ctrl+Esc or Alt+Tab).

6. Position the cursor where you want the object to appear.

7. Choose Edit ➤ Paste Special. ➤Paste Link.

8. In the As list, highlight the format you want to use for the paste link.

9. Choose OK. The linked object will appear in a graphics box.

10. Optionally, switch back to the server application and exit the application (File ➤ Exit).

To View, Edit, or Play Back a Linked or Embedded Object

1. Double-click the object. Or select (click on) the object, then choose Edit ➤ …Object from the WordPerfect menus or right-click and choose …Object from the QuickMenu.

2. If you chose menu options or QuickMenu options, a sub-menu may appear. Choose the option you want. (For OLE 2 objects, the Edit option allows in-place editing, while the Open or Activate… option usually opens the object in a sepa-rate application window.)

3. If you chose an option that allows editing, make your changes. When you're done, do one of the following:

    • If you are editing in-place (within the WordPerfect document window), click in the WordPerfect document window, outside the object.

    • If you are editing in a separate application window, choose File ➤ Exit & Return To… (or whatever com-mands normally exit the application). If you are prompted to save your changes, choose Yes.

4. If necessary, deselect the object by clicking outside the ob-ject again.

To Edit a Link

To update, cancel, or change links to paste linked objects:

1. Choose Edit ➤ Links.

2. Highlight the link you want to update, then do one of the following:

- To open the source object in a separate application window, choose Open Source. When you are done working with the object, close it normally and return to WordPerfect (for example, choose File ➤ Exit).

- To link to a different file name, choose Change Source, delete the text in the source text box, and double-click the file you want (or highlight it and choose OK).

- To update the link with any recent changes, choose Update Now.

- To change the link type, choose Automatic or Manual. Automatic links are updated whenever the file changes. Manual links are updated only when you choose Update Now.

- To break the link, choose Break Link. The object will remain in the document. However, it will no longer be linked to the source file or application.

NOTES   Upon opening a document that contains links to other files, you'll be asked for permission to update the links. Choose Yes to update the links, or No to skip the updates.

You can use normal copy and paste procedures to paste text or graphics from a WordPerfect document into another Windows application. For example, to paste a graphic from WordPerfect into a Paintbrush document, select the graphic in WordPerfect and choose Edit ➤ Copy (Ctrl+C). Open or switch to Paintbrush, then choose Edit ➤ Paste (Ctrl+V) from the application's menus.

SEE ALSO   *Chart, Draw, Graphics and Graphics Boxes, Spreadsheet/Database Import and Link, Text Art*

OPEN

Use the Open feature to open and manage files. The Open File dialog box and other similar dialog boxes use standard Windows techniques for navigating the DOS file system.

To Open a Recently-Used Document

1. Choose File from the menu bar.

2. If the file you want to open is at the bottom of the File menu, click its name. If it is not, see *To Open Any Document* below. Only the last four files you opened are listed.

To Open Any Document

1. Choose File ➤ Open, or press Ctrl+O or F4, or click the Open button in the toolbar. The Open File dialog box appears.

2. If you want to open the document as a read-only copy that cannot br changed, select (check) Open As Copy.

3. In the Filename text box, type the name of the file exactly as you typed it when you first saved it (e.g., **myfirst.wpd**) and choose OK; or type the full drive, directory, and file name (e.g, **c:\mydocs\myfirst.wpd**) and choose OK; or double-click the file name in the Filename list.

To Search for and Open a Document

If the file you're looking for is on another drive and/or directory, you can search for it and then open it.

1. Go to the Open File dialog box (step 1 and, optionally, step 2, above).

2. The list below the Filename text box initially shows all files in the current directory that have a .WPD extension. To list a different group of file names, use any of the methods below:

- If the file is on a different drive, choose the drive you want from the Drives drop-down list.

- If the file is on a different directory, choose the directory you want from the Directories list. (For example, double-click the directory you want or highlight it and press ↵.)

- To list files of a different type, select List Files Of Type and select a file type from the pull-down list.

- To specify the drive, directory, and file type all at once, type the full path name and wild cards into the Filename text box and choose OK. For example, typing **c:\mydocs\e*.*** into the box would list all files that start with *e* in the \MYDOCS directory on drive C.

3. When the list shows the file name you want to open:

- Double-click the file name you want.

- Or, press Tab or Shift+Tab until the outline is in the Filename list. Use the arrow keys or the mouse to highlight the file you want, or type the first few characters in the file name. Choose OK.

Opening More than One File

You can have up to nine files open at once. To open multiple files, use standard Windows techniques to select multiple items in the Filename list. After selecting the files, choose OK to open them.

OPTIONS   These buttons are available in the Open File dialog box:

View Opens the Viewer window, which lets you look at most files without opening them first. To see what's in a file, click on it or highlight it in the Filename list box and look at the Viewer window. You can maximize, restore, move, size, or close (Alt+F4) the Viewer window as needed. To search through the file shown in the Viewer, click on the Viewer window and press F2 to open the Find dialog box. (See the Find entry.) You can also scroll through the displayed file with the scrollbars.

QuickFinder Lets you use the QuickFinder to locate files.

File Options Lets you use these file management commands: Copy, Move, Rename, Delete, Change Attributes, Print (a file), Print File List (of displayed or selected file names in the dialog box), Create Directory, Remove Directory, Rename Directory .

QuickList Lets you edit or display the QuickList or display both the QuickList and Directories.

Setup Lets you control the sort order and file name details in the dialog box, show or hide hidden and system files, create speedup files, and decide whether the default directory changes when you use the Directories list or QuickList.

Help Provides help on file management operations.

NOTES The Open File dialog box works like many other WordPerfect for Windows dialog boxes that open or save files. You can also right-click the Filename or Directories lists, QuickList, or Viewer window and select QuickMenu options.

SEE ALSO *Combine Documents, File Management, Find, New, QuickFinder, QuickList, Save/Save As*

OUTLINE

WordPerfect's Outline feature makes it easy to number paragraphs and create hierarchical outlines. The outline is renumbered automatically as you make changes.

In the discussion below, the term *outline* refers to anything that WordPerfect should number automatically. The term *numbers* refers to numbers, bullets, heading styles, roman numerals, letters, or any other character or appearance change that WordPerfect can display in an outline item.

To Display or Close the Outline Feature Bar

In the Outline feature bar provides everything you need for automatic outlining.

- To display the Outline feature bar, choose Tools ➤ Outline.

- To hide the Outline feature bar, click its Close button.

Refer to Table IV for a complete list of Outline bar buttons and features. Note that the Options button was revised in version 6.1, and other outlining features changed slightly.

Table IV: The Outline Feature Bar's Features and Buttons

FEATURE	BUTTON	PURPOSE
Feature bar help and options	?	Provides menu options and lists keyboard shortcuts for many outlining features.
Previous level	←	Promotes an outline item to a higher level.
Next level	→	Demotes an outline item to a lower level.
Move up	↑	Moves the current paragraph or selection up without changing its level.
Move down	↓	Moves the current paragraph or selection down without changing its level.
Change to or from body text	T	Converts body text to an outline item; converts an outline item to body text.
Show family	+	Shows all members of an outline family.
Hide family	–	Hides all but the main level of an outline family.
Show outline levels	Show Outline Levels	Offers options to show outline level n or higher (where n is 1–8) or None of the outline levels.

Table IV: The Outline Feature Bar's Features and Buttons
(continued)

FEATURE	BUTTON	PURPOSE
Show level *n*	1, 2, 3, 4, 5, 6, 7, 8	Shows outline level n or higher, where n is the level indicated on the button. Excludes body text.
Show all levels	All	Shows all outline levels including body text.
Hide/show body text	Hide Body Text or Show Body Text	A toggle that either hides all body text or shows all body text.
Outline options	Options	Provides options for defining an outline, marking the end of an outline, changing a item to a specified outline level, setting an item to a specified outline number, and showing or hiding outline level icons at the left edge of the screen.
Outline style	drop-down list	Lets you choose a different outline numbering style from a drop-down list.
Close feature bar	Close	Hides the Outline feature bar.

To Create an Outline

1. Move the cursor to where the outline should begin.

2. Choose one of the methods below to start the outline:

- If the Outline feature bar isn't visible, choose Tools ➤ Outline. Choose the outline style you want from the Outline Definitions drop-down list in the Outline feature bar. Skip to step 5 below.

- If the Outline feature bar is already on the screen, click the Options button, choose Define Outline, and continue with step 3 below.

- Move the mouse pointer to the far left margin of the document window (the pointer changes to an arrow), right-click the mouse, and choose Outline from the QuickMenu. Continue with step 3.

3. Select (check) Start New Outline.

4. In the Name list, highlight the style you want and choose OK, or double-click the style name.

5. To enter text, do one of the following:

- To keep the item at the *current level*, type the text for the item. The text can be one line or an entire paragraph.

- To *demote the item* to a lower level, press Tab or click the → button in the Outline feature bar once for each level you want to move down. (You can have up to eight levels.) Type your line or paragraph of text.

- To *promote the item* to a higher level, press Shift+Tab or click the ← button in the Outline feature bar once for each level you want to move up. Type your text.

- To *assign the item to a specific level number* (between 1 and 8), click the Options button in the Outline feature bar and select Change Level. Type the level number you want and choose OK. Type your text.

6. After you've finished typing the item, you can enter another numbered item:

- If you're using an *automatic style*, press ↵ to move to the next item and insert the next numbering character (or style) at the current outline level. Depending on the style, you can press ↵ more than once to add blank lines between items and move the outline number down. (If you need more control over spacing between entries, see *Paragraph*.)

- If you're using a *manual style*, press ↵ (as many times as you want), then click the T button in the Outline feature

bar. An outline numbering character (or style) will
appear.

- To turn off automatic numbering temporarily, click the
  T button in the Outline feature bar. To turn the numbering on again, click the T button again.

7. Repeat steps 5 and 6 as needed.

8. To turn off outline numbering, click the Options button
and choose End Outline. (If a leftover outline number appears above the cursor, press Backspace as many times as
needed to remove it.)

To Change an Outline

1. Move the cursor to the item you want to change. Or, if you
want to change some feature that affects the entire outline
(such as the outline style), move the cursor anywhere in
the outline.

2. Click a button in the Outline feature bar (see Table IV, above).

To Use the Outline Editor

The outline editing tools appear at the left edge of the document
window and are visible whenever the Outline feature bar and its
Options ➤ Show Level Icons options are turned on. The hollow
numbers (*level markers*) mark the relative level of each item within
the outline. Minus (–) signs symbolize fully expanded families,
plus (+) signs indicate hidden families, and hollow T symbols (*text
markers*) denote body text.

- To *select an outline family*, move the mouse pointer to the
  highest level marker or text marker that you want to select
  (the mouse pointer will change to a two-headed vertical
  arrow), and click the left mouse button.

- To *delete an outline family*, select it, then press Delete.

- To *collapse an outline family*, move the mouse pointer to the
  marker for the topmost item that you want to collapse,
  then double-click the marker. Or, select the outline family
  and click the – (minus) button in the Outline feature bar.

- To *expand an outline family,* move the mouse pointer to the marker for the item that you want to expand, then double-click the marker. Or, select the outline family and click the + (plus) button in the Outline feature bar.

- To *move an outline family* to a new position in the outline, select (and optionally collapse) the family. Move the mouse pointer to the topmost level marker in the family and drag the marker to its new position. As you drag the marker, a horizontal bar will indicate the new position of the family. When you release the mouse button, the family will appear at the new position and the outline will be re-numbered automatically. As an alternative to dragging, you can select (and optionally collapse) the family, then click ↑ and ↓ in the Outline feature bar until you've placed the family where you want it.

- To *copy an outline family* to a new position in the outline, collapse the family (if you wish), select it, then choose Edit ➤ Copy (Ctrl+C). Click in the outline where you want to place the copied family, then press Home twice and choose Edit ➤ Paste (Ctrl+V) or press Ctrl+Shift+V (Paste Simple).

- To undo editing mistakes (if you catch the mistake immediately), choose Edit ➤ Undo (Ctrl+Z).

NOTES The numbered items in an outline are called *outline levels* and the "normal" unnumbered text is *body text.* You can freely mix outline levels with body text in any outline.

Most outlines consist of groups of related ideas, with each idea or topic placed on a level by itself. A topic and all of its subtopics compose a *family.*

WordPerfect comes with seven built-in numbering styles. A numbering style can be either automatic or manual. In the *automatic* style, WordPerfect inserts the next item number automatically, as soon as you turn outlining on and whenever you press the ↵ key at the end of a numbered line or paragraph. All the built-in styles, except the *Headings* styles, are automatic. In the *manual* style, you must tell WordPerfect explicitly when you want to enter another numbered item.

👁 **SEE ALSO** *Bullets and Numbers, Characters, Counter, Indent, Initial Codes Style, Paragraph, Styles, Tabs*

OVERSTRIKE

The Overstrike command lets you print two or more characters on top of one another to create special characters not normally available on your printer.

To Create an Overstrike

1. Move the cursor to where you want the overstrike.

2. Choose Format ➤ Typesetting ➤ Overstrike.

3. In the Overstrike dialog box, click the button to the right of the Characters text box (or press F4) and assign any font attributes you want. Attribute codes will appear in the text box, with the cursor between them.

4. Enter the overstriking characters and choose OK.

To Edit an Overstrike

1. Place the cursor just before or after an existing overstrike combination.

2. Choose Format ➤ Typesetting ➤ Overstrike.

3. Click the Previous or Next button until you locate the overstrike you want. If you get an "...Overstrike Not Found" message, choose OK to clear it.

4. Edit the overstrike combination. (If you make an editing mistake and want to return to the original overstrike character, choose Reset.)

5. Choose Close.

As a shortcut for steps 1–3 above, you can <u>V</u>iew ➤ Reveal <u>C</u>odes (Alt+F3) and double-click the [Ovrstk] code for the combination you want to change.

NOTES   Overstruck characters are printed one over the other, without advancing the print head (e.g., *0/* prints a zero with a slash through it, ø.

Overstrike character combinations available through WordPerfect's character sets should be entered using Ctrl+W key combinations rather than with Overstrike.

SEE ALSO   *Characters, Codes, Font*

PAGE BREAKS

WordPerfect paginates documents automatically by inserting a soft page break code [SPg] when you reach the bottom margin of a page, column, or label. You can control page breaks manually by inserting hard page breaks and keeping specified text together on a page.

To Insert a Hard Page Break

1.   Position the cursor where you want the page to break.

2.   Press Ctrl+↵ (or Ctrl+Shift+↵ within columns), or choose <u>I</u>nsert ➤ <u>P</u>age Break.

NOTES   A hard page break (Ctrl+↵) is also used to end one column or label and move to the next.

In Draft mode, soft page breaks appear as single horizontal lines across the screen. Hard page breaks appear as double horizontal lines across the page.

To delete hard page break codes [HPg] and codes that keep text together ([Wid/Orph:On], [Block Pro], and [Condl EOP]), turn on Reveal Codes (Alt+F3) and delete the code. (You can't delete soft page breaks.)

👁 **SEE ALSO** *Force Page, Keep Text Together, Page Numbering, Selecting Text, Suppress*

PAGE NUMBERING

The page numbering features let you specify the location and appearance of page numbers and insert page numbers within text.

To Start Page Numbering

1. Position the cursor on the page where numbering should begin.

2. Choose Format ➤ Page ➤ Numbering to open the Page Numbering dialog box.

3. From the Position pop-up list button, choose a location for page numbers: No Page Numbering (default), Top Left, Top Center, Top Right, Alternating Top, Bottom Left, Bottom Center, Bottom Right, or Alternating Bottom.

4. If you wish, choose Options and define the format and accompanying text for page, secondary page, chapter, and volume numbers, then choose OK. (See *Notes*, below.)

5. Optionally, choose Value and set page number values for page, secondary page, chapter, or volume page numbers, then choose OK.

6. Optionally, choose Font, select from various font options for the page numbers, and choose OK.

7. Choose OK to return to the document.

To Insert a Page Number in Text

1. Position the cursor where you want to insert the page number.

2. Choose Format ➤ Page ➤ Numbering.

3. Use either method below to insert the page number:

- To insert an unformatted page number, choose Value, then select (check) the Insert And Display At Insertion Point option for the type of page number you want to insert. (See *Notes*, below.)

- To insert the formatted page number, choose Options and select Insert Format And Accompanying Text At Insertion Point.

4. Choose OK twice, or choose OK and Close.

To Include Page Numbers in Headers or Footers

- Click the Number button in the Header/Footer feature bar and choose a page number option.

To Format the Page Numbers

Choose Options in the Page Numbering dialog box if you want to customize the page number format:

- You can choose a numbering method from the Page, Secondary, Chapter, or Volume pop-up list buttons. The numbering methods are Numbers, Lowercase Letter, Uppercase Letter, Lowercase Roman, and Uppercase Roman.

- You can use the Format And Accompanying Text box to
  format the page number text. Position the cursor and type
  any text you want to appear. When you want to insert a
  page numbering place- holder, click Insert and select
  Page Number, Secondary Number, Chapter Number, or
  Volume Number.

NOTES Document page numbers appear only if you request it. Page numbers will appear in Page view or Two-Page view
and in the printed document. Use the Suppress command to prevent
page numbers from printing on a certain page (for example, a title
page) without interrupting the numbering sequence.

You can have four levels of page numbers: page number, secondary
(section) number, chapter number, and volume number. WordPerfect increments the page and secondary numbers automatically.
Chapter and volume page numbers stay the same unless you
change them manually.

SEE ALSO *Font; Headers, Footers, and Watermarks; Initial
Codes Style; Suppress; View*

PAPER SIZE

Use the Paper Size feature to select from the extensive list of Word-
Perfect's predefined paper sizes or to create non-standard paper
sizes for documents such as labels and envelopes.

To Select, Create, Edit, or Delete a Paper Size

1. Position the cursor where the paper size should take effect.

2. Select the printer you want to use (File ➤ Print ➤ Select)
   and return to the document window.

3. Choose For_mat_➤ _P_age ➤ Paper _S_ize to open the Paper Size dialog box.

4. If you want to select, edit, or delete a paper size, highlight the paper size you want.

5. Choose one of these options:

- To _select_ the highlighted paper size, choose _S_elect (or double-click the desired paper size). You'll return to the document window.

- To _create_ a new paper size, choose C_r_eate.

- To _edit_ the highlighted paper size, choose _E_dit.

- To _delete_ the highlighted paper size, choose _D_elete, then choose _Y_es. Skip to step 7.

6. Define or change the paper size (see _Options_, below). When you're done, choose OK.

7. To select another option, return to step 4. To return to the document window, choose _C_lose.

OPTIONS   These options are available in the Create Paper Size and Edit Paper Size dialog box for both Windows and WordPerfect printer drivers.

Paper Name   The name you want to appear in the _P_aper Definitions list.

Type   Choose a paper type from the list of paper types.

Size   Choose a predefined paper size from the _S_ize dropdown list, or choose User Defined Size and enter a custom size. The default paper size is Letter ($8\frac{1}{2}\times 11$ inches).

Location   Varies according to printer, but usually includes Manual Feed and Default.

Orientation   Select or deselect Rotated _F_ont and _W_ide Form as needed. The sample page in the dialog box provides a graphical view of your selection.

Text Adjustments If your printer isn't positioning a document correctly, you can adjust the position vertically (T<u>o</u>p) or horizontally (Sid<u>e</u>). Enter the distance you want to adjust the text in each direction. This option may require some trial-and-error.

NOTES When you select a paper size, WordPerfect inserts a [Paper Sz/Typ] code at the top of the current page.

Definitions are printer-specific. Once you create a definition for a specific printer, you don't have to redefine it.

You can insert more than one paper size code in your document.

Place Paper Size definitions in the document Initial Codes Style of a form file (see *Merge Operations*).

SEE ALSO *Binding, Envelope, Initial Codes Style, Labels, Merge Operations, Print, Template*

PARAGRAPH

In WordPerfect, a paragraph is any text that ends with a hard return [HRt]. You can use several features to format the appearance of your paragraphs.

To Format Paragraphs

1. Position the cursor where formatting should start, or select the paragraphs.

2. Choose Fo<u>r</u>mat ➤ P<u>a</u>ragraph ➤ <u>F</u>ormat.

3. Specify the settings you want:

• To change the first line indent, choose <u>F</u>irst Line Indent and enter a measurement.

- To change spacing between paragraphs, choose Spacing Between Paragraphs and enter the number of lines you want between paragraphs.

- To adjust the paragraph margins relative to the page margins, choose Left Margin Adjustment or Right Margin Adjustment and enter a measurement.

- To restore all the default settings, choose Clear All.

4. Choose OK.

To use the ruler bar to specify first line indent or paragraph margins, follow these steps:

1. Display the ruler (View ➤ Ruler Bar or Alt+Shift+F3).

2. Position the cursor where formatting should start, or select the paragraphs.

3. Drag markers at the top of the ruler as follows (the status bar will display the name and position of the marker being moved):

- To change the first line indent, drag the indent marker (top left triangle) to a new position.

- To change the left or right paragraph margin, drag the appropriate paragraph adjustment marker (bottom left or right triangle) to a new position.

To Add Paragraph Borders and Fill

1. Position the cursor where formatting should start, or select the paragraphs.

2. Choose Format ➤ Paragraph ➤ Border/Fill.

3. Choose a border or fill option as described below:

- To change the border style, click the Border Style button or drop-down list and click the style you want. Or, select a border style other than No Border or <None> and choose Customize Style to set up a custom border.

- To change the fill style, click the Fill Style button or drop-down list and click the style you want. You can also choose colors from the Foreground and Background buttons.

- To turn the border and fill off, click the Off button.

4. To apply the changes to the current paragraph only, select (check) Apply Border To Current Paragraph Only. To apply the changes to all paragraphs below the cursor position (assuming you didn't select text in step 1), deselect (clear) this option.

5. If necessary, choose OK to return to your document.

To Remove Paragraph Borders and Fill

1. Repeat steps 1 and 2 of the procedure above.

2. Choose Off.

 NOTES Use Indent features to indent individual paragraphs (see the Indent entry).

SEE ALSO *Indent, Lines and Borders, Margins, Ruler*

PASSWORD

You can add passwords to your documents to protect them from unauthorized use. A password-protected document cannot be opened or printed from WordPerfect unless the correct password is entered.

To Create or Change a Password

1. Open (File ➤ Open or Ctrl+O) or create (File ➤ New or Ctrl+N) the document.

2. Choose File ➤ Save (Ctrl+S) for new documents or File ➤ Save As (F3) for new or previously saved documents.

3. If you haven't specified a file name for the document, type one into the Filename text box.

4. Select (check) Password Protect and choose OK.

5. Type the password. The characters of the password will appear as asterisks when you type them.

6. Choose one of the protection methods below (new in version 6.1):

- To use case-sensitive passwords that *aren't* readable in older versions of WordPerfect, choose Enhanced Password Protection.

- To use case-insensitive passwords that *are* readable by older versions of WordPerfect, choose Original Password Protection.

7. To set the protection chosen in step 6 as the default method, select (check) Use As Default; otherwise, deselect (clear) this option.

8. Choose OK.

9. Retype the password to confirm your entry and choose OK.

10. To activate the protection, close the file (File ➤ Close or Ctrl+F4).

To Remove a Password

1. Open the document (File ➤ Open or Ctrl+O).

2. When prompted, type the password and choose OK.

3. Choose File ➤ Save As (F3).

4. Deselect (clear) the Password Protect check box.

5. Choose OK.

6. When asked if you want to replace the file, choose Yes.

7. Close the file (File ➤ Close).

 NOTES Passwords don't protect the file from being deleted, copied, moved, or renamed, nor do they provide high-level security or encryption.

To change a password, open the file, choose File ➤ Save As, and continue with step 3 of the "To Create or Change a Password" procedure.

SEE ALSO *File Management, Save/Save As*

PATH AND FILE NAME

Use this feature to insert the current file name or path and file name anywhere in a document. This information is especially useful in page headers and footers.

The file information displayed will instantly reflect the new file or file and path if you copy, move, save, or rename the file.

To Insert the File Name or Path and File Name

1. If you want to show the file information in a new file, save the file (File ➤ Save).

2. Position the cursor where you want the information to appear.

3. Choose Insert ➤ Other.

4. To insert the current file name, choose Filename. To insert the full path name of the file, choose Path And Filename.

WordPerfect inserts a [Filename] code at the cursor location.

NOTES   See *Save/Save As* for a discussion on file naming rules.

SEE ALSO   *Date/Time; File Management; Headers, Footers, and Watermarks; Save/Save As*

POWER BAR

The power bar (shown below) provides shortcut buttons for many WordPerfect operations.

| Times New Roman | 12 pt | Styles | Left | 1 0 | Tables | Columns | 100% |

To Display or Hide the Power Bar

- Choose View ➤ Power Bar.

This toggle option displays the power bar (if it was hidden) or hides it (if it was visible). You can also hide the power bar by right-clicking it and choosing Hide Power Bar.

To Find Out What a Button Does

Move the mouse pointer to the button and look at the title bar at the top of the screen. Also look for a QuickTip description near the mouse pointer.

To Use the Power Bar

- To choose a power bar button, click it. Or, click the button and drag or click to highlight the selection you want.

- You can go directly to the dialog boxes for many features by double-clicking their power bar buttons.

- To customize the power bar (add, delete, and move buttons), right-click the power bar and choose Options. Or
  choose Edit ➤ Preferences and double-click Power Bar.
  See the Preferences entry for more information.

 **SEE ALSO**   *Hide Bars, Preferences, Ruler, Status Bar,*
Toolbar

PREFERENCES

When you install WordPerfect, many aspects of appearance and
behavior are predefined. You can use the Preferences options to
change these settings as desired.

To Change Default Preferences

1. Choose Edit ➤ Preferences.

2. Double-click the icon for the preference you want to
change, or highlight the icon and press ↵, or choose an option from the Preferences menu in the dialog box. (See
Options, below.)

3. Complete the dialog box for the selected preference.

4. Choose OK or Close as necessary to return to the Preferences dialog box.

5. Choose Close to return to your document.

To Go Directly
to a Specific Preferences Dialog Box

1. Using your mouse, point to the toolbar, power bar, scroll
bar, menu bar, ruler bar, status bar, or Reveal Codes.

2. Right-click the mouse and choose Preferences (or Options) near the bottom of the QuickMenu.

OPTIONS The following Preferences options are available:

Display Controls these features of the document window: D̲ocument (what to show on the document window, and what units of measurement to use; S̲how ¶ (which "invisible" symbols appear on-screen and whether they initially appear in documents); View/Z̲oom (default view and zoom size); Reveal C̲odes (Reveal Codes font, size, color, window size, and other appearance options, and whether Reveal Codes initially appears in documents); R̲uler bar (behavior and appearance of the ruler and whether it initially appears in other documents); Merge (appearance of merge codes).

Environment Controls a variety of items, including user information for comments and document summaries, formatting prompts, deletion confirmations, and warning beeps.

File Controls default directory locations, file extensions, file names, and whether the QuickList is updated with changes. You can set file preferences for D̲ocuments/Backup, Templates, S̲preadsheets, D̲atabases, Me̲rge, P̲rinters/Labels, Hy̲phenation, G̲raphics, and M̲acros.

Summary Controls default subject text and descriptive type on document summaries, whether to display descriptive file names in file management dialog boxes, and whether to create a document summary upon saving or exiting.

Toolbar Lets you S̲elect, C̲reate, E̲dit, Copy, Re̲name, and Delete toolbars and customize the toolbar appearance and position. Each button can execute a program, feature, play a keyboard script, launch a program or play a macro.

Power Bar Lets you edit the power bar, select which buttons appear on it, reset it to the default buttons, and customize its appearance.

Status Bar Lets you edit the status bar, select what information it shows, reset it to the default information, and customize its appearance.

Keyboard Lets you S̲elect, C̲reate, E̲dit, Copy, Re̲name, and D̲elete keyboards. The selected keyboard controls how each key behaves. A key can do nothing, display a text character, execute a program feature, play a keyboard script, launch a program, or play a macro.

Menu Bar Lets you Select, Create, Edit, Copy, Rename, and Delete menus. Each menu item can execute a program feature, play a keyboard script, lanch a program, or play a macro.

Writing Tools Controls which writing tools (Grammatik, Spell Checker, and Thesaurus) appear in the Tools menu.

Print Controls default print preferences for relative size of fonts (size attribute ratio), number of copies printed and how copies are generated, print quality, print color, the color printing palette used, whether graphics are printed and whether documents are reformatted for the currently selected printer on open.

Convert Controls default conversion settings, including delimiters for fields and records, characters used to enclose text strings, characters to strip during import, code pages, the conversion preferences for some other file formats, and Windows Metafile conversion options.

You can use the Help button in each preferences dialog box to learn more about each preference setting.

 SEE ALSO *Entries for features mentioned above.*

PRINT

Use the Print dialog box to print any portion of any document.

To Print the Currently Displayed Document

- Press Ctrl+P, choose File ➤ Print or click the Print button on the toolbar and choose Print.

To Print Any Portion of Any Document

1. If you want to print a portion of the current document , select that portion.

2. Choose File ➤ Print to get to the Print dialog box.

3. If you wish to select a different printer, choose Select and
use the Windows Default Printer option or Specific Printer
drop-down list to select a printer. Then choose Select.

4. Under Print Selection, choose what you want to print
(Full Document, Current Page, Multiple Pages, Selected
Text, Document Summary, or Document On Disk.

5. Optionally, choose the number of copies you want to print
and how to generate the copies. For Generated By, you can
choose WordPerfect (printed pages will be collated, but
printing can be slow) or Printer (generally faster, but
printed pages aren't collated).

6. Under Document Settings, choose a Print Quality (the
lower the quality, the faster the print) and Print Color (if
you're using a color printer). If you want to print only the
text of your document, select Do Not Print Graphics.

7. You can also choose Options from the Print dialog box,
then select from the following options and choose OK to
return to the Print dialog box.

Print Document Summary   Prints the document summary, if the current document has one.

Booklet Printing   Prints the document as a booklet or
pamphlet, if you've subdivided each page into two columns (see the Subdivide Page entry).

Print In Reverse Order   Prints from last page to first
(handy if your printer normally stacks printed pages in
reverse order).

Print Odd/Even Pages   Useful for printing pages back-to-
back on a non-duplex printer. That is, you can print the
odd-numbered pages first, then put those pages back in
the printer and print only the even-numbered pages.

Output Bin Options If your printer has a deluxe output bin, you can activate that bin's Sort, Group, and Jogger capabilities. If you have multiple bins, you can select a bin as well.

Print Document Graphically New in version 6.1, this feature lets you print without downloading your fonts to the printer. This sometimes helps if you're having trouble printing white text on black, and it prevents graphics lines from printing through graphics boxes that they intersect (this is especially handy if you're using separator lines between columns in a multicolumn document).

8. Choose Print when you've made all of your selections and are ready to print.

9. If you opted to print Multiple Pages, you'll be prompted for a range of pages. You can enter specific pages separated by a comma or indicate a range of pages with a hyphen. For example, **3,5,20-30** would print page 3, then page 5, then pages 20 through 30. Choose Print again to start printing.

10. If you selected Document On Disk, type (or select) the name of the document you want to print in the Filename text box. Enter any specific pages you want printed or accept the default (all pages), then choose Print again to start printing.

To Send a Fax from WordPerfect

You must have a Fax board installed according to the manufacturer's instructions. Then, to fax a WordPerfect document directly from disk or from your screen, follow the steps above, but choose your Fax board driver as the printer to use in step 3. Complete the rest of the steps normally, and respond to any prompts that your Fax driver displays on the screen.

SEE ALSO *Booklets and Pamphlets, Columns, Graphics and Graphics Boxes, Graphics Lines and Borders, Preferences*

QUICKCORRECT

The QuickCorrect feature fixes misspelled words, corrects some capitalization errors and problems with spaces, replaces straight quotes with "SmartQuotes," and substitutes abbreviations with expanded text. All this happens instantly, as you type!

To Turn QuickCorrect On and Off

1. Choose Tools ➤ QuickCorrect (Ctrl+Shift+F1). The Quick-Correct dialog box will open.

2. To replace misspellings and abbreviations as you type, select (check) Replace Words As You Type. To prevent instant replacement, deselect (clear) this option.

3. To control certain typing errors within sentences or at the end of sentences, and to configure SmartQuotes, choose Options. Complete the QuickCorrect Options dialog box (see *Options*, below) and choose OK.

4. Choose Close.

To Add Replacement Words

1. Choose Tools ➤ QuickCorrect.

2. In the Replace text box, type the mispelled word or abbreviation that should be replaced automatically. To change an existing replacement word, click on that word in the list below the Replace text box.

3. In the With text box, type in or edit the word you want to use as a replacement.

4. Click the Add Entry button (if you're adding a new word) or the Replace Entry button (if you're replacing an existing word).

5. Repeat steps 2– 4 as needed. When you're done, choose Close.

To Delete Replacement Words

1. Choose <u>T</u>ools ➤ QuickCorrect.

2. In the list below the <u>R</u>eplace text box, highlight the word you want to delete.

3. Choose <u>D</u>elete Entry, and then <u>Y</u>es.

4. Repeat steps 2 and 3 as needed. When you're done, choose <u>C</u>lose.

Options You can choose and customize several options in the QuickCorrect Options dialog box (<u>T</u>ools ➤ QuickCorrect ➤ <u>Op</u>tions). For options with check boxes, select (check) the option to turn on the automatic replacement; deselect (clear) the option to turn off the automatic replacement.

Capitalize First Letter Determines whether WordPerfect automatically replaces a lowercase letter at the beginning of a sentence with a capital letter.

Correct TWo IRregular CApitals Determines whether WordPerfect automatically replaces words that have initial double uppercase letters (e.g., *THe*) with single uppercase letters (e.g., *The*).

Double Space To Single Space Determines whether WordPerfect automatically replaces two adjacent spaces in a sentence with one space.

End Of Sentence Corrections Determines which corrections WordPerfect should make to spaces that follow an end-of-sentence punctuation mark (period, exclamation point, or question mark). Your options are <u>N</u>one (make no changes), change <u>S</u>ingle Space To Two Spaces, or change <u>T</u>wo Spaces To Single Space.

Turn On Single Quotes Determines whether WordPerfect replaces straight open and closed single quotes with the quotes shown in the <u>O</u>pen and C<u>l</u>ose text boxes. (Use the drop-down lists to select different <u>O</u>pen and C<u>l</u>ose single quotes.)

Turn On Double Quotes Determines whether WordPerfect replaces straight open and closed double quotes with the quotes shown in the O<u>p</u>en and Clos<u>e</u> text boxes. (Use the drop-down lists to select different O<u>p</u>en and Clos<u>e</u> double quotes.)

Use Regular Quotes With Numbers Determines whether WordPerfect uses straight quotes with numbers at all times (e.g., 35" or 1950s' greatest hits). If you deselect this option, Word-Perfect will use the SmartQuotes instead of regular quotes (assuming you've also turned on the appropriate single quotes and double quotes).

 **SEE ALSO**   *Abbreviations, Characters, Macros, Spell Checker*

QUICKFINDER

QuickFinder can search rapidly through files and QuickFinder indexes for certain words, phrases, or patterns. The result will be a list of files that contain the information you searched for.

For fastest searching, create and use QuickFinder indexes.

To Open the QuickFinder

You can get to the QuickFinder using either method below:

- Go to any Open File, Select File, or Save As dialog box (for example, choose File ➤ Open). Click the QuickFinder button. (We'll assume you're using this method.)

- Start from the Program Manager and double-click the QuickFinder File Indexer icon in the WPWin 6.1 group window.

To Create a QuickFinder Index

1. Choose File ➤ Open ➤ QuickFinder.

2. Choose Indexer. If prompted, select a directory for storing the index and choose OK.

3. Choose Create.

4. Type an index name and choose OK.

5. To add a file or files to the index, type the file, directory name, or wildcard pattern into the Add Directory (And File Pattern) text box. (Alternatively, you can choose Browse, then select the file or directory you want.)

6. To include subtrees of a selected directory, select (check) Include Subtree.

7. Choose Add. (If you add a file or directory accidentally, highlight it in the Directories To Index list and choose Remove.)

8. Repeat steps 5–7 as needed.

9. To choose the amount of detail in the index, choose Options, select the options you want, and choose OK (See *Options*, below).

10. To generate the index, choose Generate. After the index is complete, choose OK, choose Close twice, then choose Cancel.

To Manage QuickFinder Indexes

1. Choose File ➤ Open ➤ QuickFinder.

2. Choose Indexer.

3. Highlight an index name in the Index Names list.

4. Take one of the actions below:

- To regenerate the highlighted index, choose Generate. Then select Update Index With New Or Modified Files or select Index All Files. Choose OK until you return to the QuickerFinder File Indexer dialog box.

- To edit the highlighted index, choose Edit. Proceed as for creating an index above (start with step 5).

- To get information about the index, to delete, rename, or move the index, to import an index that someone else created, or to change the index preferences, choose the Options button and select the option you want.

5. Repeat steps 3 and 4 as needed.

6. Choose Close in the QuickFinder File Indexer dialog box, Close again in the QuickFinder dialog box, then choose Cancel.

To Search with QuickFinder

1. Choose File ➤ Open ➤ QuickFinder.

2. In the Search For text box, type the word, phrase, or pattern you want to search for. You can use the Operators button to create a more complicated search pattern, and the Concepts button to include alternative word forms in your search. You can leave this text box blank to search for any files that match the other criteria specified in the QuickFinder dialog box, regardless of the text in those files.

3. Use the Search In pop-up list button to specify where QuickFinder should search (Directory, Subtree, Disk, or QuickFinder Index). If you choose Disk or QuickFinder Index, select the drive or the name of the index in the drop-down list box.

4. In the _Path(s) /Pattern(s) text box, specify a file pattern.

5. To limit the search to files that were created or changed in a specific date range, use the pop-up list button, text boxes, and calendar buttons next to the File Date Range option.

6. To limit the search to WordPerfect documents only, select (check) WordPerfect Documents Only.

7. Choose Find.

8. If QuickFinder finds a match, the Search Results List dialog box will open. You can then do any of the following:

- To view files without opening them, choose View and click on or highlight files in the Search Results list.

- To return to the QuickFinder dialog box, choose Quick-Finder.
- To change the sort order of files, choose Sort Setup.
- To do file management tasks, choose File Options. (See the File Management entry.)
- To save the search results, select (check) Save Search Results.
- To rearrange the Search Results list, drag the heading buttons. You can use the buttons to move, resize, and delete columns. Click the < and > buttons to scroll columns to the left or right.

OPTIONS   The Options button in the QuickFinder dialog box provides these capabilities:

Estimated Relevance Ranking Ranks the documents in order of relevancy to your search criteria. It is faster, but less precise than the Full Word Count Relevance method.

Full Word Count Relevance Also ranks the documents in order of relevancy. However, this option uses the actual number of times the search text was found in the document to determine the relevancy. It takes longer, but is more precise than Estimated Relevance Ranking.

No Summary Fields Hides document summary fields.

Default Summary Fields Shows the default document summary fields. You can include these fields in your search.

All Summary Fields Shows all document summary fields. You can include these fields in your search.

Last Search Results Returns to the most recent list of saved Search Results.

Clear Clears the Search For text box.

Load Search Query Lets you load a saved search query.

Save Search Query Lets you save a search query.

Delete Search Query Lets you delete a saved search query.

NOTES If you change the contents of indexed files or directories, you should regenerate the appropriate QuickFinder indexes before using them again. The KickOff program offers a handy method for updating QuickFinder indexes on a regular basis (see *KickOff*).

SEE ALSO *File Management, Find, KickOff, Open, Save/ Save As*

QUICK FORMAT

Quick Format lets you quickly format other text in your document with the same fonts and Paragraph styles that are in effect at the cursor position.

To Quick-Format Text

1. Place the cursor in or select text that has the font or Paragraph style you want to copy.

2. Choose Format ➤ QuickFormat, right-click and choose QuickFormat, or click the QuickFormat button in the WordPerfect toolbar.

- To copy only the fonts and print attributes to other text, choose Characters.

- To copy fonts, print attributes, paragraph formats, and styles to other text, choose Headings. This option creates an *Auto QuickFormat style*, and assigns it to the current paragraph and any other *related paragraphs* you click on in step 5 below. (See *Notes*, below.)

3. Choose one of the options below:

Characters Copies only the fonts and attributes to other selected text.

Headings Copies the fonts and attributes as well as paragraph formatting and styles to a new style named Auto QuickFormat*x* (where *x* is a number, and *Auto* indicates the automatic behavior of this style). WordPerfect then places a [Para Style: Auto QuickFormat *x*] code at the start of the current paragraph.

4. Choose OK or press ↵. The mouse pointer will change to a paint roller shape.

5. Apply the formatting to other, related paragraphs as follows:

- If you chose Characters in step 3, use your mouse to select the text you want to quick-format. WordPerfect will copy codes from the original selected text into the selected text that you quick-format.

- If you chose Headings, click the paragraph you want to quick-format. When you release the mouse button, WordPerfect will apply the appropriate Auto Quick-Format*x* style to the paragraph, and insert a corresponding [Para Style: Auto QuickFormat*x*] code at the beginning of the paragraph.

6. Repeat step 5 until you've reformatted as many portions of text as you want.

7. To turn off QuickFormat, repeat step 2.

To Update Quick-Formatted Paragraphs Automatically

If you chose Headings in step 3 of the above procedure, any changes to the attributes of *any* paragraph that was quick-formatted will instantly update the appearance of all related paragraphs that you clicked in step 5.

To Prevent Automatic Updates to Quick-Formatted Paragraphs

1. Put the cursor in the paragraph you want to update.

2. Choose Format ➤ QuickFormat, right-click and choose QuickFormat, or click the QuickFormat button in the WordPerfect toolbar.

3. Choose Discontinue.

4. Choose one of the following options:

Current Heading Discontinues automatic updates on the current paragraph only. This option breaks the link between the current paragraph and its related paragraphs by assigning a new (non–automatic).

QuickFormat style to the current paragraph (e.g., [Para Style: QuickFormat5]). The Auto QuickFormat style (e.g., [Para Style: Auto QuickFormat4]) assigned to the related paragraphs is not affected.

All Associated Headings Discontinues automatic updates in this paragraph and all its related paragraphs. This option assigns a new (non-automatic)

QuickFormat style (e.g., [Para Style: QuickFormat5]) to the current paragraph and to all its related paragraphs.

5. Choose OK.

6. Change the appearance of the paragraph as desired.

 SEE ALSO *Font, Paragraph, Styles, Template*

QUICKLIST

The QuickList lets you assign descriptive, easy-to-remember names for frequently-used directory and file names. You can select a QuickList entry instead of typing file and directory names into dialog boxes.

Many QuickList entries are created automatically when you define directory and file locations in the File Preferences dialog box.

To Use the QuickList

1. Go to the Open File, Select File, or Save As dialog box (e.g., choose File ➤ Open).

2. If the QuickList isn't visible in the dialog box, choose QuickList ➤ Show Both (or QuickList ➤ Show QuickList).

3. To select an entry in the QuickList, click it. Or choose QuickList and highlight the entry you want. This fills in the Filename or Directory Name text box with the file, directory, or wildcard name assigned to the QuickList entry.

4. Complete the dialog box as required by whatever operation you chose in step 1.

To Add, Change, and Delete QuickList Entries

1. Go to the Open File, Select File, or Save As dialog box (e.g., choose File ➤ Open). If necessary, select QuickList ➤ Show QuickList or QuickList ➤ Show Both, so that you can see the QuickList. Show Both is usually the best choice.

2. Take any of the actions below:

    • To create a new entry, choose QuickList ➤ Add Item. In the Directory/Filename text box, type a directory name, file name, or wildcard pattern; or use the file button on the dialog box to locate and fill in a directory name. In the Description text box, enter a description for the entry (or accept the description that appears automatically). Choose OK.

    • To edit an existing entry, highlight the entry and choose QuickList ➤ Edit Item. Proceed as for creating a new entry.

- To delete an entry, highlight the entry, choose QuickList ➤ Delete Item then choose Yes.
- To print the currently selected Quicklist entry, or all QuickList entries, choose QuickList, ➤ Print QuickList, complete the dialog box, and choose Print.

3. Repeat step 2 as needed.

4. Choose Cancel to close the Open File, Select File, or Save As dialog box.

SEE ALSO *File Management, Open, Preferences, Print, Save/ Save As*

QUICKMENU

WordPerfect displays a QuickMenu when you right-click a certain area of the screen (see Notes, below). Options on the QuickMenu are relevant to the area of the WordPerfect screen you click.

To Use a QuickMenu

1. Point to a "hot spot" area (see Notes, below) on the document window or a file management dialog box and then right-click the mouse.

2. To choose an option from the menu and click on it with the left or right mouse button, type the option's underlined letter, or press ↑ and ↓ as needed to highlight the option, and then press ↵.

 **NOTES** The following hot spot areas offer QuickMenus: normal document text, far left edge of document window, Reveal Codes, scroll bars, status bar, toolbar, power bar, menu bar, ruler bar, tables, graphics boxes and lines, comments, headers, footers, and lists in the file management dialog boxes.

SEE ALSO *Menus, Mouse*

REPEAT

The Repeat feature lets you repeat a keystroke, command, or macro a specified number of times. Not all actions can be repeated.

To Repeat an Action

1. Move the cursor to the location where an action will be repeated.

2. Choose Edit ➤ Repeat.

3. Optionally, specify the number of times to repeat the action.

4. If you want the number to be the new default setting, choose Use As Default.

5. Choose OK.

6. Press a key, choose a menu option, click a button on the toolbar, or run a macro.

SEE ALSO *Macros, Menus, Toolbar*

REPLACE

Use Find And Replace to locate any sequence of characters or codes and change it to something else.

To Replace Text or Codes

1. To be safe, save the document (File ➤ Save).

2. Move the cursor to where replacement should start or select only the text to be affected.

3. Choose Edit ➤ Find And Replace or press F2.

4. Complete steps 2–5 of the Find procedure (see *Find*). In these steps, you specify the text to search for in the Find text box (step 2), choose options from the Direction menu to indicate a search direction (step 3), select options from the Action menu to specify what happens when a match occurs (step 4), and choose options from the Options menu to control where the search should begin (step 5).

5. If you want to limit the number of changes made, choose Options ➤ Limit Number Of Changes.

6. Move the cursor to the Replace With text box, and specify the replacement text. You can type text and WordPerfect characters (Ctrl+W), and choose Replace options (Case, Font, or Codes). If you want to *delete* the search string, delete all the text in the Replace With text box (or leave the setting at <Nothing>).

7. Start the replacement as described below:

- To find and highlight the next (or previous) match, *without* making any changes, choose Find.

- To find and highlight the next (or previous) match without making any changes, choose Find.

- To replace the currently highlighted match then highlight the next (or previous) match, choose Replace.

- To replace all matches at once (up to the limit specified by Options ➤ Limit Number Of Changes), choose Replace All.

8. When you're done making changes, choose Close.

NOTES If you are unhappy with the changes, you may be able to undo them by choosing Edit ➤ Undo (Ctrl+Z) or by clicking the Undo button in the toolbar until all your changes are reversed. Or, if you saved your document in step 1 above, you can choose File ➤ Close ➤ No to discard your changes; then open the file again.

SEE ALSO *Characters, Close, Codes, Find, Open, Undo/Redo*

REVEAL CODES

WordPerfect uses codes to implement most formatting features. These codes are hidden unless you open the Reveal Codes window, which appears in the lower part of your screen.

To Turn Reveal Codes On and Off

Use one of the following methods:

- Choose View ➤ Reveal Codes (Alt+F3).

- Right-click in the center of the document editing area and choose Reveal Codes from the QuickMenu.

- Or, if Reveal Codes is on, right-click the Reveal Codes window and choose Hide Reveal Codes.

To Use the Reveal Codes Window

You can take any of these actions when the Reveal Codes window is visible:

- To *edit text*, position the cursor in the document window or the Reveal Codes window and edit normally.

- To see a brief *description of a code*, point to it with your mouse and look at the title bar at the top of the screen.

- To *delete a code*, click on it or move the cursor just to the right of the code. Press Backspace (if the cursor is just to the left of the code, press Delete instead), or drag the code above the Reveal Codes window and release the mouse button. Deleting one paired code deletes both codes.

- To go directly to a *dialog box* for editing the code, double-click the code. (This works for many codes.)

- To *move a single code*, delete the code. Position the cursor where you want the code to reappear and choose Edit ➤ Undelete (Ctrl+Shift+Z), then choose Restore.

- To *copy or move one or more single codes*, select the code(s) and choose Edit ➤ Copy (Ctrl+C) or Edit ➤ Cut (Ctrl+X). Position the cursor where you want the code(s) to reappear and choose Edit ➤ Paste (Ctrl+V). You can only move or copy single codes only, not paired codes.

- To customize the Reveal Codes window, right-click the Reveal Codes window and choose Preferences.

- To resize the Reveal Codes window, move the mouse pointer to the dividing line between the normal document window and the Reveal Codes window (the pointer changes to a two-headed vertical arrow). Now drag the divider up or down and release the mouse button.

NOTES The example below shows a screen with the Reveal Codes window open. The top section is the normal document window. The lower portion, which displays codes and text, is the Reveal Codes window.

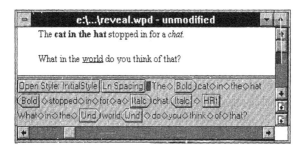

The Reveal Codes cursor is a rectangle that appears just to the left or right of characters and codes as you move through the document window. The cursors on both screens are at exactly the same place in the document, and both move together. Codes usually appear as buttons to distinguish them from text.

You can use Reveal Codes to check for proper formatting, delete a code, or make sure relevant codes are included when you select text (see the Selecting Text entry).

SEE ALSO *Codes, Delete, Document Window, Preferences, Selecting Text, Undelete, Windows*

RULER

The ruler (shown in Figure 5) provides shortcuts for formatting paragraphs, margins, tab stops, columns, and tables. You can also right-click or double-click the ruler or its markers to reach relevant dialog boxes.

The ruler has two sections: the paragraph, margins, tables, and columns area on top, and the tab stops on the bottom. (Figure 5 does not show the tables and columns markers. These appear at the top of the ruler.)

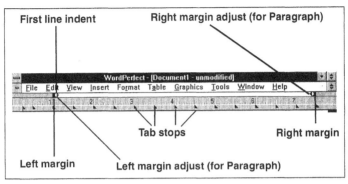

First line indent   Right margin adjust (for Paragraph)

Tab stops   Right margin

Left margin   Left margin adjust (for Paragraph)

Figure 5: The Ruler

To Turn the Ruler On and Off

- Choose <u>V</u>iew ➤ <u>R</u>uler Bar (Alt+Shift+F3) to display or hide the ruler.

- Or, right-click the ruler and choose <u>H</u>ide Ruler Bar (to hide the ruler).

To Use the Ruler to Set Tab Stops

General procedures for using the ruler to set tab stops are listed below. See the specific entries listed in the See Also section below for other ways to use the ruler.

1. Move the cursor to where you want to change the settings, or select text to limit your changes to a block.

2. Take one of the actions below:

- To set a new tab stop, right-click the mouse in the tab stops area, select a tab type, then click the mouse at the correct spot on the bottom of the ruler. A new tab stop marker will appear.

- To delete a tab stop, drag its marker down off the ruler.

- To move a tab stop, margin, paragraph margin, or first-line indent, or to resize a column, drag the appropriate marker to its new position. The status bar at the bottom of the screen will indicate what you are changing and its current position. Release the mouse button when the marker is positioned properly.

NOTES To customize the ruler, right-click it and choose Preferences.

SEE ALSO *Codes, Columns, Margins, Paragraph, Prefer-ences, Tables, Tabs*

SAVE/SAVE AS

Documents are held only in the computer's memory until you save them. To prevent loss of work, you must save your changes before you close a document window, exit WordPerfect, or turn off your computer.

To Save a Document

1. Choose File ➤ Save (Ctrl+S) or File ➤ Save As (F3), or click the Save button in the toolbar.

2. If you chose File ➤ Save for a file that was previously saved, WordPerfect will save the file under the previous name and won't prompt further. If the file is new or you chose File ➤ Save As, continue with the remaining steps.

3. In the Filename text box, enter the file name or full path name for the document. You can also use any technique discussed in the File Management entry to help you fill in the text box.

4. If you want to save the file in a non-WordPerfect format (e.g., WordStar or ASCII text), choose the format from the Save File As Type drop-down list.

5. Choose OK.

6. If the file name already exists on disk, WordPerfect will ask if you want to replace the existing file. Choose Yes to replace it or No to return to step 3.

NOTES   File names can have up to eight characters, plus a period and a one- to three-letter extension. Full path names include a drive letter, the name of each directory above the file, separated by backslashes (\), and the file name.

Never use spaces in path names, file names, or extensions. Avoid using extensions with special meanings to DOS, Windows, or WordPerfect (such as .COM or .EXE).

Unless you enter a full path name, the file is saved in your current or default directory. If you omit the extension, WordPerfect uses the default extension defined in File Preferences.

Sample file names are   MEMO   MEMO.WPD   MYSTUFF.1

Sample path names are   D:\MEMOS\MYSTUFF.1   A:MEMO.WPD

You can use Save As to add, change, or remove passwords from a file (see the Password entry).

When you close a document window (File ➤ Close or Ctrl+F4) or exit WordPerfect (File ➤ Exit or Alt+F4), WordPerfect will prompt you to save changes if you haven't done so yet. Choose Yes to save the changes, No to discard changes, or Cancel to return to the document.

See the Master Document entry to learn about saving master documents and subdocuments.

SEE ALSO   *Combine Documents, Document Summary, Exit, File Management, Master Document, Password, Path and Filename, Preferences*

SELECTING TEXT

Selecting text lets you identify text to be moved, copied, printed or deleted, and also lets you activate appearance attributes (bold, italic), styles, and other features *after* you've typed the text. Selected text appears highlighted on screen.

To Select Text with the Mouse

1. Position the I-beam at one end of the text you wish to select.

2. Hold down the left mouse button and drag the mouse pointer to the other end of the text. The text will be highlighted.

3. Release the left mouse button.

See the Mouse entry for other selection methods.

To Select Text with the Keyboard

1. Optionally, turn on Reveal Codes (Alt+F3) so you can be sure appropriate codes are included or excluded from the selection.

2. Position the cursor at one end of the text.

3. Use any of these techniques to select the text:

- Hold down Shift and use the arrow, Home, End, or other cursor-positioning keys to extend the selection.
- Choose options from the Edit ➤ Select menus.
- Press F8 and use cursor-positioning keys to extend the selection.
- Press F2 (Find And Replace), choose Action ➤ Extend Selection, type the text or codes to extend the selection to, and choose Find Next.

NOTES After selecting text, you can choose almost any formatting option that WordPerfect offers. Options that aren't available for selected text will be dimmed in the menus.

If you type a character while a block is selected, the entire block will be replaced with that character.

To "unselect" selected text without performing an operation, move the cursor, click the left mouse button, or press F8.

SEE ALSO *Cursor, Find, Mouse*

SHORTCUT KEYS

Use keystroke combinations from the keyboard to accomplish common tasks quickly. You can customize the keyboard layout to create shortcut keys (see *Preferences*).

NOTES Shortcut keys are listed on the menus to the right of the command names.

To see a complete list of shortcut keys assigned to a keyboard that you've created, choose Edit ➤ Preferences and double-click Keyboard. Highlight the keyboard you want to look at and choose Edit.

SEE ALSO *Menus, Preferences*

SORTING AND SELECTING

Use Sort to arrange information into a more meaningful order or to extract or isolate specific information from documents. You can sort lines, paragraphs, table rows, parallel columns, and merge data file records.

To Sort and Extract

1.   If you'll be selecting records, make a copy of the file first for safety (File ➤ Save As).

2.   Position the cursor anywhere in the document text (to sort the entire document or a file on disk) or inside a table or columns (to sort the table or columns). Or select the text or rows you want to sort.

3.   Choose Tools ➤ Sort (Alt+F9).

4.   Specify the Input File (current document or a file on disk).

5.   Specify the Output File (current document or a file on disk). When specifying a document on disk, be careful not to use the original file or any other file you care about.

6.   To sort uppercase letters before lowercase letters, choose Options and select (check) Uppercase First. To do a dictionary sort where uppercase and lowercase letters are treated equally, deselect (clear) Options ➤ Uppercase First.

7.   To enable the Undo command for use immediately after sorting or isolating information to the current document, choose Options and select (check) Allow Undo. This can be slower, but is generally safer. To disable the Undo command, deselect (clear) Options ➤ Allow Undo.

8.   If you want to use one of the predefined sorts or selections, highlight the appropriate entry in the Defined Sorts list, and continue with step 11.

9.   If you want to define your own sort key and/or selection criteria, do one of the following:

•   To update one of the predefined sorts or selections, highlight the appropriate entry in the Defined Sorts list, then choose the Edit button. The Edit Sort dialog box appears.

•   To copy one of the predefined sorts or selections and update the copy, highlight the appropriate entry in the

Defined Sorts list, then choose the Copy button. The
Edit Sort dialog box appears.
To create a new sort or selection from scratch, choose
the New button. The New Sort dialog box appears.

10. In the Edit Sort or New Sort dialog box, define the Sort
Name, type of record to sort, sort key definitions, and any selection criteria. Then choose OK to return to the Sort dialog
box. (See *To Define a Sort Key* and *To Select Records*, below.)

11. To start the sort or selection, choose Sort.

If your sort didn't work out as expected, and you selected Allow
Undo in step 7, press Ctrl+Z immediately to undo the changes.
(This works only when you're sorting output to the current
document.)

To Delete a Sort or Selection

1. Choose Tools ➤ Sort (Alt+F9).

2. Highlight the sort or selection you want to delete in the
Defined Sorts list.

3. Choose the Delete button and answer Yes when prompted
for confirmation.

4. Choose Close.

To Create or Edit a Sort/Selection Definition

Sort/selection definitions specify the sort keys and selection criteria. These reusable definitions (new in version 6.1) appear in the
Defined Sorts list in the Sort dialog box.

Sort keys specify which piece of the record to sort by. You can have
up to nine sort keys (Key1, Key2, Key3, …, Key9). Key1 has first
priority, Key2 second priority, and so on. To create a definition:

1. Go to the New Sort or Edit Sort dialog box (step 9 under
"To Sort and Extract," above).

2. Optionally, specify a sort definition name in the Sort Name text box. This name will appear in the Sort Definition list. The name <User Defined Sort> is assigned to new definitions automatically, but you can change it as needed.

3. Optionally, specify the type of records to sort in the Sort By area. Your choices are Line, Paragraph, Merge Record, Table Row, and Column. (See *Notes*, below.)

4. Define the sort keys in the Key Definitions area as follows:

- To add a new key to the bottom of the list, choose the Add key button.

- To insert a key, click where the new key should appear and choose Insert Key.

- To delete a key, click the key to be deleted and choose Delete Key.

- To select the key you want to change, use the Add Key or Insert Key button (as described just above), or click anywhere on the key, or press Alt plus the key number (e.g., Alt+1). The selected key number will be marked with a > character.

5. Specify the key *Type:* either Alpha (numbers and letters) or Numeric (numbers, dollar signs, commas, and periods only).

6. Specify the *Sort Order:* either Ascending (A–Z, 0–9, negative to positive) or Descending (Z–A, 9–0, positive to negative).

7. Specify which column, field, line, and word to sort by in each key (as appropriate). These items are numbered from left to right within the record. To number from right to left, use a negative number. For example, Word -1 is the last word, Word -2 is the second-to-last word, and so on.

To Select Records

Define your sort keys as explained above. Then use the Select Records text box in the New Sort or Edit Sort dialog box to define selection criteria that will select (isolate) specific records. *Warning: Records that don't*

*meet the the Select Records criteria will be deleted if you extract them to the cur-
rent file, or if you overwrite the input file with the extracted version of the file!*

To extract records without sorting them first, select (check) Select
without sorting.

Each selection criterion in the Select Records text box has these
components:

• A *key* specified as "key*n*" where *n* is a number (e.g., *key1*).
  Use "*keyg*" instead of a key number for a global selection
  where any field can qualify (e.g., keyg=Bermuda will
  match "Bermuda" in any field).

• A *selection operator*. The operators are | (OR), & (AND), =
  (equal), <> (not equal), > (greater than), < (less than), >=
  (greater than or equal), and <= (less than or equal).

• A *value* to match. Values can be numbers and/or letters.

You can combine key statements, such as *Key1>=Jones & Key1<=Smith*.
Selection is done from left to right unless you use parentheses for
grouping, as in *key5=male & (key1=Smith | key1=Jones)*.

Sample selection criteria are shown in Table V.

Table V: Sample Selection Criteria

CRITERIA	MEANING
key1=Smith	key3=Arizona	Selects all Smiths and all Arizona records.
key1=Smith&key3=Arizona	Selects all Smiths in Arizona
key3=Arizona	Selects all Arizona records.
key3<>Arizona	Selects all resisdents that don't live in Arizona

Table V: Sample Selection Criteria (continued)

CRITERIA	MEANING
key3>M	Selects residents in states that start with M or later in the alphabet (e.g., Maryland, Michigan, Nebraska and Washington, but not Arizona, California, or Georgia)
key3<M	Selects residents in states with names that are earlier than M in the alphabet (e.g., Arizona, California, and Georgia, but not Maryland, Michigan, Nebraska, or Washington.
key4<=92123	Selects residents with zip codes less than or equal to 92123 in key4.
key4>=92123	Selects residents with zip codes greater than or equal to 92123 in key4.
key3=Utah & key1=Smith ∣ key1=Brown	Selects Smiths in Utah and all Browns.
key3=Utah & (key1=Smith ∣ key1=Brown)	Selects Smiths and Browns in Utah.

NOTES *Records* are the lines, paragraphs, rows in parallel columns or tables, or text blocks to be sorted. Each record can be further broken down into columns, fields, lines, and/or words.

Fields are separated by tabs or indents in lines and paragraphs, and by ENDFIELD codes in merge records. In tables, each column is a field. Records can contain many fields. Each corresponding field should contain the same type of information.

There are five different kinds of records:

Line   Each line is a record that ends with a hard return [HRt]. Records are divided into fields and words.

Paragraph   Each paragraph is a record. Paragraphs must end with at least two hard returns [HRt]. Records are divided into lines, fields, and words.

Merge Record (non-tabular merge file)   Records are separated by ENDRECORD codes. Records are divided into fields, lines, and words.

Table Row   Each row is a record. Records are divided into columns, lines, and words.

Column (parallel columns)   Each record is a row of columns. Records are divided into columns, lines, and words.

Lines are separated by hard or soft returns.

Words are separated by spaces, forward slashes (/), or hard hyphens (Ctrl+–) within a line or field. To select multiple words for sorting as if they were single words, place a hard space (Ctrl+spacebar) between the words that should be treated as a single word. This is useful when sorting names like "Edward Merriweather III" and "John Jones" by last name.

Columns are separated by hard column breaks [HCol] entered by pressing Ctrl+↵.

Codes within a record will be sorted along with the record. This may affect the appearance of text between paired codes.

To sort text according to a certain language, insert a Language code before the text you're sorting (see *Language*).

To sort dates, treat the month, day, and year as separate words and divide dates with forward slashes (07/08/94) or hard hyphens (07-08-94). To enter a hard hyphen, press Ctrl+-.

 **SEE ALSO**   *Columns, Hyphenation, Language, Merge Operations, Spaces (Hard and Soft), Tables*

SOUND

If your computer has sound capabilities, you can add sounds to your WordPerfect documents. Two methods are available: Object Linking and Embedding (see *Object Linking and Embedding*) and WordPerfect's Insert ➤ Sound feature (described below).

To Add a Sound Clip

1. Move the cursor to where you want to put the sound clip.

2. Choose Insert ➤ Sound ➤ Insert.

3. Optionally, enter a name for the sound clip in the Name text box.

4. In the File text box, type the name of the file that contains the sound clip, or use the file button to locate the sound clip. (Sound clips are often stored in c:\windows or its subdirectories.)

5. To have the sound change if you change the sound file on disk and to keep your document smaller, select Link To File On Disk. To prevent the sound from changing if you change the sound file on disk, choose Store In Document (your document will be larger).

6. Choose OK. A sound clip comment will appear at the cursor position.

To Play a Sound

Click the sound clip icon, or sound clip comment box, or follow the steps below:

1. Choose Insert ➤ Sound to open the Sound Clips dialog box.

2. Highlight the sound clip you want to play in the Sound Clips In Document list.

3. Click the Play button. You can also use the Rew (Rewind), FF (Fast Forward), and Stop buttons and the Playback Controls scroll bar to listen to the sound again.

4. Choose Close when you're done.

OPTIONS   These additional options are available in the Sound Clips dialog box:

Record   Opens the Windows Sound Recorder, which lets you record sounds, create special sound effects, and save sounds to disk. See your Windows documentation for information.

Edit Desc.   Lets you change the name (description) of a sound clip.

Transcribe   Lets you play back sounds while you work in the document window. Use this option to type into your document while listening to the sound (this is like taking dictation). You can also reach this option by right-clicking the sound comment icon and choosing Transcribe from the QuickMenu.

Delete   Lets you delete the highlighted sound clip.

Save As   Lets you save to disk a sound clip that's stored in the document.

 **SEE ALSO**   *Hypertext, Macros, Object Linking and Embedding*

SPACES (HARD AND SOFT)

You can insert hard or soft spaces between words. Use hard spaces [HSpace] to have more than one word treated as a single word for formatting, hyphenation, and sorting. Use soft spaces to treat each word separately.

To Insert a Soft or Hard Space

1. Position the cursor where you want to insert the space.

2. For a *soft space*, press the spacebar. For a *hard space*, press Ctrl+spacebar.

 **SEE ALSO** *Hyphenation, Sorting and Selecting*

SPELL CHECKER

Spell Checker can identify and replace spelling errors, repeated words, words containing numbers, and capitalization errors. You can also have Spell Checker suggest words that fit a particular pattern and you can automatically add replacement words to the QuickCorrect dictionary.

To Start a Spell Check

1. Optionally, move the cursor to the word or page you want to check, or select a block of text.

2. Choose Tools ➤ Spell Check (Ctrl+F1), or click the Spell Check button on the Word Perfect toolbar.

3. Optionally, choose Check from the Spell Checker menu bar and select the scope of the spell check (Word, Sentence, Paragraph, Page, Document, To End Of Document, Selected Text, Text Entry Box, Number Of Pages).

4. If you wish, select or deselect items on the Options menu. (See *Options*, below.)

5. If necessary, choose Start to begin the spell check.

6. Respond to prompts that appear (see next section).

To Correct Misspelled Words

During a spell check, Spell Checker will highlight any word that it can't find in the main or supplementary dictionaries. The Suggestions list will show possible replacements for the misspelled word. You can then choose from the options below:

- Select the correct word in the Suggestions list and click Replace.

- Click the To pop-up list button and choose the dictionary you want to add the word to. Select Add to add the word to the dictionary.

- Select Skip Once to skip this occurrence of the word.

- Select Skip Always to skip all occurrences of the word.

- Edit the word in the Replace With text box and click Replace.

- List other suggestions. Enter a word or word pattern (see Notes, below) in the Replace With text box, then choose Suggest.

- Click in the document window and make changes. Click Resume to resume spell checking.

- Click QuickCorrect to add the highlighted word and the word shown in the Replace With text box to the correction list in the QuickCorrect dictionary (new in version 6.1). Future typos involving the misspelled word will be corrected automatically as you type (assuming you've checked the Replace Words As You Type option in QuickCorrect).

To Use Different Spell Checker Dictionaries

WordPerfect uses a built-in main dictionary (wt6oen.mor), a supplementary dictionary (usually named wtspelus.sup), and the document supplemental dictionary (stored in the document). The main dictionary usually is stored in c:\office\shared\wpc20. The wtspelus.sup dictionary usually resides in c:\windows. You can create supplementary dictionaries of your own and buy additional main dictionaries from WordPerfect Corporation. (The dictionary names given here assume a single-user system using U.S. English dictionaries. Network and foreign language dictionary names will be different.)

To Choose a Different Dictionary

1. Choose Dictionaries from the Spell Checker menu bar.

2. Choose Main or Supplementary.

3. Choose an option below:

- To *create* a new supplementary dictionary or *insert* an existing dictionary into the Dictionaries In Search Order list, highlight the position where the dictionary name should appear, and choose Add or Create. Respond to additional prompts.

- To edit a dictionary, highlight the dictionary name in the list and choose Edit. You can then add, edit, or delete keywords that Spell Checker will skip, replace, or offer alternatives for during a spell check.

- To delete a dictionary from the chain, highlight the dictionary name and choose Delete, then Yes.

- To specify a different language for the chain, choose Language, select the language, and choose OK. The language module must already be installed according to the manufacturer's instructions.

4. When you're ready to return to the Spell Checker dialog box, choose Close.

OPTIONS You can choose these items from the Options menu before starting a spell check:

Words With Numbers Enables or disables checking for embedded numbers in words.

Duplicate Words Enables or disables checking for double words.

Irregular Capitalization Enables or disables checking for irregular capitalization.

Exhaustive Checking   Enables or disables display of all possible suggestions in languages where limited suggestions are usually displayed.

Auto Replace   When deselected, Spell Checker will prompt before changing a word that you've previously designated as "auto-replace." When selected, Spell Checker will auto-replace without prompting first.

Auto Start   When selected, spell checking starts as soon as you start Spell Checker. (For selected text, spell checking begins immediately, even if you haven't selected Auto Start.)

Recheck All Text   When selected, Spell Checker will recheck all parts of the document for spelling errors. When deselected, Spell Checker will not recheck portions that it has already checked during the current session (new in version 6.1).

Document Dictionary   When selected, Spell Checker will not stop at misspelled words that you previously added to the supplementary dictionary that's attached to the current document. When deselected, Spell Checker will stop at misspelled words that you previously added to this dictionary.

QuickCorrect Dictionary   Enables or disables lookups in, and updates to, the QuickCorrect dictionary (new in version 6.1).

Beep on Misspelled   Enables or disables a beep sound when Spell Checker finds a misspelled word.

NOTES   You can enter word patterns in the Replace With text box, and then choose Suggest to see a list of words that "sound like" the pattern you entered.

A word pattern is composed of characters and wildcards. Use a question mark (?) to represent a single character and an asterisk (*) to represent multiple characters. For example, *chil?* results in *child, Chile, chili,* and *chill*; while **kmarks* retrieves *bookmarks* and *pockmarks*.

To temporarily disable the writing tools, including Spell Checker, move the cursor to where you want to disable the tools, or select a block of text. Choose Tools ➤ Language, check the Disable Writing Tools… box, and choose OK.

You can also run Spell Checker by double-clicking the Spell Checker icon in the WPWin 6.1 group window in Program Manager.

(eye icon) **SEE ALSO** *Grammatik, Hyphenation, Language, Preferences, QuickCorrect, Thesaurus*

SPREADSHEET/DATABASE IMPORT AND LINK

You can import (copy) or link information from a spreadsheet, database, or delimited text file into your WordPerfect document. Linked files will be updated in your WordPerfect document automatically whenever they change in the underlying data file. Imported files won't be updated in your document when the underlying files change.

To Import or Link Data

1. Move the cursor to where you want the data to appear in your document.

2. Choose Insert ➤ Spreadsheet/Database.

3. To import the data, choose Import. To link the data, choose Create Link.

4. Use the Data Type pop-up list button to select the type of data to import or link. You can choose Spreadsheet, any of several database formats, or Delimited Text formats.

5. Use the Import As or Link As pop-up list button to select the format of the data in the WordPerfect document. Your options are Table, Text, and (non-tabular) Merge Data File.

6. In the Filename text box, specify the name of the data file to import or link, or use the file button to locate the file. Or, if you chose an ODBC data type, specify the Data Source and Table.

7. Depending on the Data Type, you can further tailor the imported/linked data:

- For *spreadsheets*, you can select Named Ranges or specify a Range.

- For *databases*, you can select (check) the Fields you want and and choose whether to Use Field Names As Headings. You can even define a Query to limit the imported/linked data to specific conditions in up to three fields.

- For *delimited text*, you can change the Field and Record delimiters, the characters that surround (Encapsulate) strings of text, and the characters to Strip upon import.

8. Choose OK to import or link the data.

OPTIONS These options are also available on the Insert ➤ Spreadsheet/Database menu:

Edit Link Lets you edit the link for the data the cursor is in. After choosing this option, follow steps 4–8 above to edit a link.

Update Lets you update all data links at once.

Options Lets you choose whether to update the links when you retrieve the document and whether to show the link icons.

NOTES A spreadsheet range is a rectangular section of a spreadsheet file. To specify a range, enter the cell addresses of the top-left and bottom-right corners, separated by a colon, period, or two periods (e.g., A1:F35, A1.F35, or A1..F35). If the spreadsheet file has named ranges, the names will appear in the list box and you can select the name instead of typing the cell addresses.

To break a link but leave the data in your document, turn on Reveal Codes (Alt+F3) and delete the appropriate [Link] code.

Data that's linked or imported as text will be separated into columns by tabs and into rows by hard returns.

To set the default delimiters and characters for imported delimited text files, choose Edit ➤ Preferences and double-click Convert.

 **SEE ALSO** *Merge Operations, Object Linking and Embedding, Preferences, Tables*

STATUS BAR

The status bar appears at the bottom of the WordPerfect window to provide information about the current status of your WordPerfect document. Initially the bar shows whether you're in Insert mode or Typeover mode, whether a macro is being recorded, the currently selected printer, whether text is selected, the current date and time, and the location of the cursor within the document. You can display, hide, and customize the status bar.

To Display or Hide the Status Bar

- Choose View ➤ Status Bar (to display or hide the bar).

- Or, right-click the status bar and choose Hide Status Bar (to hide the bar).

To Customize the Status Bar

- Choose Edit ➤ Preferences and double-click the Status Bar icon, or right-click the status bar and choose Preferences.

 **SEE ALSO** *Hide Bars, Preferences*

STYLES

Styles let you apply consistent formatting to your text. Any changes that you make to a style will be reflected automatically in any text formatted with that style.

To Create a Style

1. Choose Format ➤ Styles, press Alt+F8, or double-click the Styles button in the power bar. The Style List dialog box opens.

2. To choose which styles appear in the Style List and where style changes will be saved, choose Options ➤ Setup, select any options below, then choose OK.

- *Display Styles From* options control which styles appear in the Style List. Your options are Current Document, Default Template, Additional Objects Template, and System Styles. System styles are WordPerfect's built-in styles (you can edit these, but you cannot delete them).

- *Default Location* options determine where WordPerfect saves your style changes. You can choose Current Document (the default), Default Template, or Additional Objects Template.

3. Choose Create.

4. In the Style Name text box, type a name for the style. (Do not assign style names that are already used for other styles in other templates and documents.)

5. In the Description text box, type a description of the style.

6. Choose a style type from the Type pop-up list. Your options are Character (Paired), Paragraph (Paired), Paragraph (Paragraph (paired-auto) or Document (Open). (See *Options*, below.)

7. If you wish, choose options that control what the Enter (↵) key does in a Character or Paragraph style (it's often easiest to skip this step). See "To Control the Enter Key," below.

8. To have the style activate some new format at its end, select (check) Show 'Off Codes'.

9. To define the formatting codes and text, choose Contents. If you checked Show 'Off Codes' in step 8, enter codes that turn the style on before the [Codes To The Left Are ON…] code, and codes that turn it off after that code. See "To Enter Style Codes in the Contents Box," below.

10. When you're done, choose OK to return to the Style List.

11. Choose Close to return to your document.

To Apply a Style

1. Move the cursor to where the style should begin, or select a block of text.

2. Choose Format ➤ Styles or press Alt+F8. Or click the Styles button in the power bar and select a style (skip step 3).

3. Highlight the style you want and choose Apply, or double-click the style.

To Enter Style Codes in the Contents Box

Use any technique below to enter formatting text and codes in the Contents box:

- Choose formatting features from the menus or use the usual shortcut keys.

- Type any text or special characters (Ctrl+W) that you want WordPerfect to insert automatically.

- To delete a code, move the cursor to it and press Delete or drag the code out of the Contents box.

- To see what your style will look like without the hidden codes, deselect Reveal Codes. To redisplay the codes in the Contents box, select Reveal Codes again.

- To insert an existing style into the one you're creating, choose Format ➤ Styles or press Alt+F8, highlight a style from the Style List, and choose Apply.

- To insert a page break [HPg] into the style, press Ctrl+↵. To insert a hard return [HRt], press Shift+↵. To insert a tab ([Left Tab]), press Ctrl+Tab.

To Control the ↵ Key

When creating or editing a style in the Contents box, you can control the behavior of the ↵ key as follows:

- To have ↵ insert a hard return without turning the style off, deselect (clear) Enter Key Will Chain To (for Character styles only).

- To have ↵ move the cursor past a style and turn the style on again, select Enter Key Will Chain To and choose <Same Style> from the drop-down list.

- To have ↵ move the cursor past the style, select Enter Key Will Chain To and choose <None> from the drop-down list.

- To have ↵ move the cursor past the style, then turn on another style, select Enter Key Will Chain To and choose the style you want to turn on next from the drop-down list.

OPTIONS   These style types are available:

Character (paired)   Like most paired codes, formats any number of characters between the [Char Style] codes. You can usually turn off a character style by pressing → .

Paragraph (paired)   Formats text from the cursor position to the first hard return that it finds. Usually, pressing ↵ turns a paragraph style off and back on again. To turn the style off, press Alt+F8 and apply the <None> style, or click the Styles button in the power bar and choose <None>.

Paragraph (paired-auto) Same as a Paragraph (paired) style, except that any changes you make to an entire paragraph that's formatted with the Paragraph (paired-auto) style will affect all other paragraphs that are formatted with the same style. This type of style is created automatically if you choose the Headings option when quick-formatting paragraphs (see *QuickFormat*).

Document (open) Useful for formats that affect an entire document. Once turned on, a document style stays on until some other style (or code) takes over.

These additional options are available in the Style List dialog box (Format ➤ Styles):

QuickStyle Copies basic formatting codes from the cursor position into a new style. After choosing this option, specify the style name, description, and type and choose OK. (This is the same as choosing QuickStyle from the styles button in the power bar.)

Edit Lets you edit the highlighted style. You can also edit a style by turning on Reveal Codes (Alt+F3) and double-clicking the appropriate style code in the Reveal Codes window.

Options Leads to these options: Setup (lets you choose which styles appear in the Style List and where style changes are stored); Copy (lets you copy the highlighted style to the current document, current template, or additional objects template); Delete (deletes the highlighted style); Reset (resets the highlighted system style to its default codes); Retrieve (lets you retrieve system styles, user-defined styles, or both from a saved file or style library); Save As (lets you save system styles, user-defined styles, or both to a style library file).

NOTES Styles can be saved to the current document (default), default template, or additional objects template.

Style lists in subdocuments are combined into the master document.

SEE ALSO *Codes, Master Document, Outline, Preferences, Quick Format, Template*

SUBDIVIDE PAGE

You can subdivide pages into columns and rows (rectangles). Each rectangle is treated as a separate page. For example, each sheet of 8 ½"× 11" paper that's divided into three columns and four rows will contain 12 rectangles, with each rectangle treated as a separate page.

Entering text on subdivided pages is similar to entering text on labels. You can see this effect in Page view and Two-Page view.

To Subdivide Pages

1. Choose Format ➤ Page ➤ Subdivide Page.

2. Specify the Number Of Columns you want.

3. Specify the Number Of Rows you want.

4. Choose OK.

To Edit Text on a Subdivided Page

- Type and edit text normally. WordPerfect will start a new "page" automatically when the current page is filled.

- To force a new rectangle (page) to appear at the cursor position, press Ctrl+↵ or Ctrl+Shift+ ↵ (in columns).

- To move the cursor from page to page, press Alt+PgUp and Alt+PgDn, or use any feature described in the Go To entry.

To Turn Off Subdivided Pages

- Move the cursor to where you want to disable the feature, then choose Format ➤ Page ➤ Subdivide Page ➤ Off.

NOTES If you wish to reduce the margins on subdivided pages, choose Format ➤ Margins.

To add borders or fill patterns to every square, choose Format➤ Page ➤ Border/Fill.

SEE ALSO *Booklets and Pamphlets, Go To, Labels, Columns, Graphics Lines and Borders, Margins, Page Breaks, View*

SUPPRESS

You can turn off (suppress) automatic page numbering or repeating elements (headers, footers, or watermarks) to prevent them from appearing on the current page.

To Suppress Page Numbering or Repeating Elements

1. Position the cursor where you want to suppress the feature.

2. Choose Format➤ Page ➤ Suppress.

3. Select (check) whatever feature(s) you want to suppress, or choose All to suppress all features at once.

4. If you've turned on automatic page numbering and want to print a page number at the bottom center of the page, select Print Page Number At Bottom Center On Current Page.

5. Choose OK.

To Turn the Suppressed Features Back On

- Repeat steps 1 and 2 above, then deselect the appropriate check boxes, and choose OK. Or remove the appropriate [Suppress] code in Reveal Codes.

SEE ALSO   *Headers,   Footers,   and   Watermarks;   Page Numbering*

TABLE OF AUTHORITIES

A Table of Authorities (ToA) is a list of citations in a legal document. The table is typically divided into sections according to the type of citation (Cases, Constitutional Provisions, Authorities, etc.). The document itself generally contains a *full form* citation (the first reference in the document) and a *short form* citation (an abbreviated way to show all subsequent references to the same authority).

To Display or Hide the ToA Feature Bar

Table of Authorities features are available when the Table of Authorities feature bar is visible.

- To display the feature bar, choose <u>T</u>ools ➤ Table Of <u>A</u>uthorities.

- To hide the feature bar, click the <u>C</u>lose button in the feature bar.

To Set Up Citations

Repeat these steps for each authority that you cite:

1.   Use the full form procedure to mark the full-form citation of the authority, edit the full-form text (if necessary), and assign a "nickname" (the short form) to that authority.

2.   Use the short form procedure to mark all remaining references to the same authority.

After marking all the citations, define the appearance and location of each section of the table, then generate the table.

To Mark a Full Form Citation

1.   Display the ToA feature bar.

2.   Select the long form of the citation.

3.   Click the Create Full Form button in the feature bar.

4.   In the Section Name text box, type a section name where the citation will appear or choose a section name from the drop-down list.

5.   In the Short Form text box, type in or accept the suggested short form name (the short form name must be unique to this full form).

6.   Choose OK.

7.   Edit the full form text that appears in a new editing window. If necessary, you can use the Short Form and Section boxes in the feature bar to reassign the short form name or section. Choose Close when you're done editing the full form.

To change the full form citation later, click the Edit Full Form button in the ToA feature bar, highlight the short form name of the citation and choose OK (or double-click the name). Repeat step 7 above.

To Mark a Short Form Citation

1.   Display the ToA feature bar.

2.   Select the short form you want to mark from the Short Form drop-down list in the feature bar.

3.   Position the cursor just after the short form text you want to mark. (You can choose Edit ➤ Find And Replace or press F2 to locate text quickly.)

4.   Choose Mark from the feature bar.

5.   Repeat steps 3 and 4 for the remaining short forms of this citation in the document.

To Define the ToA

1.   Display the ToA feature bar.

2.   Move the cursor to where you want the section to appear.

3.   Optionally, press Ctrl+⏎ to insert a page break.

4.   Optionally, position the cursor, type a section heading, and press ⏎.

5.   Click the Define button in the feature bar.

6.   Optionally, do one of the following to create, edit, or delete ToA sections:

- To *change the definition* of a section, highlight the section name and choose Edit. You can change the name and any appearance options you want (see Options, below). Choose OK.

- To *create a new ToA definition*, choose Create. In the Name box, type a name for the section. Choose any appearance options you want. Choose OK.

- To *delete a section definition*, highlight the section and choose Delete, then choose Yes.

- To *retrieve a list* of section definitions from another document, choose Retrieve, specify the document name, and choose OK. Select (check) the definitions to include and choose OK.

7.   To insert the section definition into the document at the cursor location, highlight the section name and choose Insert.

8.   Repeat steps 2–7 for each section in the ToA.

9.   Optionally, use Page Numbering (Format ➤ Page ➤ Numbering ➤ Value) to restart page numbering for pages that follow the ToA.

To Generate the ToA

1.   Choose Tools ➤ Generate from the menu bar, press Ctrl+F9, or click Generate in the Table of Authorities feature bar.

2.   Choose OK.

OPTIONS   You can choose any of the options below when creating or editing a ToA section definition:

Name   The ToA Section name.

Position   Lets you define where the page number appears with respect to the text of the citation.

Page Numbering   Lets you define the format of the page number.

Underlining Allowed   When selected (checked), any underlining in the text you marked will be included in the ToA. When deselected, underlining is removed in the ToA.

Use Dash To Show Consecutive Pages   When selected (checked), a dash indicates consecutive page numbers. When deselected, each page number in a range is listed separately.

Use As Default   Uses the format of the current section as the default for new sections.

Change   Lets you change the style of the ToA entries.

NOTES   You can create a ToA for an individual document or a master document, but be sure to place the ToA definition in the master document, *not* in a subdocument.

To delete a citation entry, turn on Reveal Codes (Alt+F3) and delete the appropriate [ToA] code. Then regenerate the ToA.

SEE ALSO *Find, Generate, Index, List, Master Document, Page Numbering, Table of Contents*

You can create a table of contents with up to five levels of indentation. This involves three basic steps. First, mark table of contents entries in your document. Second, define the table of contents location, number of levels, and appearance. Third, generate the table of contents.

To Display or Hide the ToC Feature Bar

Table of Contents features are available when the Table of Contents feature bar is visible.

- To display the feature bar, choose Tools ➤ Table Of Contents.

- To hide the feature bar, choose the Close button in the feature bar.

To Mark ToC Entries

1. Display the Table of Contents feature bar.

2. Select the word or phrase you want to include in the ToC. (You can choose Edit ➤ Find And Replace or press F2 to locate words and phrases quickly.)

3. Click the Mark *n* button in the feature bar to assign the text to a table of contents level (*n* is a level number from 1 to 5).

Repeat steps 2 and 3 until you've marked all the entries you want.

To Define the ToC

1. Move the cursor to where you want the table of contents to appear (usually at the start of your document).

2. Optionally, type a title for the table of contents and press ↵

3. Display the Table of Contents feature bar.

4. Click the Define button in the feature bar.

5. Choose formatting options from the Define Table Of Contents dialog box. You can define the number of levels and the appearance of each level in the ToC (see Options, below).

6. Choose OK to return to the document window.

7. Optionally, press Ctrl+↵ to insert a page break.

8. Optionally, use Page Numbering (Format ➤ Page ➤ Numbering ➤ Value) to restart page numbering for pages that follow the ToC.

To Generate the ToC

1. Choose Tools ➤ Generate from the menu bar, press Ctrl+F9, or click Generate in the Table of Contents feature bar.

2. Choose OK.

OPTIONS Choose any of these formatting options in the Define Table of Contents dialog box.

Number Of Levels (1–5) Specifies the number of levels to include in the ToC.

Position Lets you define where the page number appears with respect to the text of the table of contents entry.

Styles Lets you change the style for each level of the ToC.

Page Numbering Lets you define the format of the page number.

Display Last Level In Wrapped Format Select (check) to wrap the lowest level of the ToC. Deselect to prevent wrapping.

NOTES To delete a table of contents entry in the document, turn on Reveal Codes (Alt+F3) and delete the appropriate [Mrk Txt ToC] code. Then regenerate the ToC.

SEE ALSO *Find, Generate, Index, Lists, Master Document, Page Numbering, Styles, Table of Authorities*

TABLES

The tables feature lets you organize text and pictures into neat rows and columns. You can also add shading and lines to emphasize parts of the table, and you can remove all or some of the lines, as in the examples presented below.

To Create a Table

1. Choose Table ➤ Create, press F12, or double-click the Table QuickCreate button in the power bar.

2. Specify the number of Columns and Rows.

3. If you want to format the table automatically, choose Table Expert (new in version 6.1). Then, highlight a style from the Available Styles list, decide whether the table style should update automatically if the table size changes, and choose Apply.

4. Choose OK.

To quickly create a plain table, move the mouse pointer to the Table QuickCreate button in the power bar and then drag out a table with the number of columns and rows you want. (See "To Format a Table with the Expert," below for details about formatting tables automatically.)

To Type in a Table

Move the cursor into the table and type normally. To move the cursor within the table, click any cell with your mouse or use the Tab, Shift+Tab, Alt+←, Alt+ →, Alt+↑, Alt+↓, and arrow keys.

To Select Text within a Table

Drag the mouse pointer through the cells you want to select, or hold down the Shift key while using the cursor-positioning keys.

To Display or Hide Row/Column Indicators

- Put the cursor in the table, then right-click and choose Row/Column Indicators, or click the Row/Column Indicators button in the Tables toolbar or Table Formula feature bar. (This toggle feature is new in version 6.1.)

To Select Table Cells, Columns, or the Entire Table

1. Move the mouse pointer to any line within the table until the pointer becomes a vertical or horizontal arrow. Or, if you will be using the row/column indicators to select a row or column, put the cursor anywhere in the table.

2. Do one of the following:

   - To select the cell, click once.

   - To select the row or column, click twice (double-click). Or, click the appropriate row or column indicator.

   - To select the entire table, click three times (triple-click). Or, click the top-left corner on the row/column indicators.

To Resize Columns

To size columns to fit the text they contain:

1. Use one of the methods below to tell WordPerfect which column(s) to resize, and how wide the column(s) should be:

   - To resize one column as wide as its widest line of text, put the cursor in that column.

   - To resize a column as wide as a specific cell's line of text, select whichever cell should determine the fit.

   - To resize multiple columns as wide as each column's longest line of text, select the columns.

2. Right-click the selection and choose Size Column To Fit from the QuickMenu, or click the Size Column To Fit button in the Tables toolbar.

To resize columns by dragging:

1. Move the mouse pointer to the vertical line in the table or to the line in the row/column indicator that's just to the right of the column you want to resize. The mouse pointer will change to cross-hairs.

2. Drag the column line to the left (to narrow the column) or to the right (to widen the column). The Position indicator at the right of the status bar will indicate the current position of the line as you drag. For added control while dragging:

• To adjust the width of the column next to the one you're resizing, do not hold down any keys while dragging.

• To resize the remaining columns proportionally to the column you're resizing, hold down Shift while dragging.

• To have all the remaining columns retain their original size, hold down Ctrl while dragging.

3. When the column is the desired width, release the mouse button.

To size columns more precisely:

1. Move the cursor into the column you want to resize, or select the columns you want to resize.

2. Choose Table ➤ Format ➤ Column, or press Ctrl+F12 and choose Column.

3. Set the Width option to the width you want. If you do not want the column(s) to change size to accommodate changes to the width of other columns, select (check) Fixed Width. You can also increase or decrease the Left and Right margins within the column(s).

To Insert Rows and Columns

• To insert a row above the current row, press Alt+Ins.

• To insert a row below the current row, press Alt+Shift+Ins or move the cursor to the last cell in the table and press Tab.

- To insert several rows or columns, move the cursor to where you want to insert row(s) or column(s) and choose Table ➤ Insert (or right-click the table and choose Insert). Specify the number of Columns or Rows to insert and whether you want them placed Before or After the cursor position. Choose OK.

To Delete Rows and Columns

- To delete the row at the current cursor position, press Alt+Del.

- To delete several rows or columns, move the cursor to where you want to delete row(s) or columns(s) and choose Table ➤ Delete (or right-click the table and choose Delete). Specify the number of Columns or Rows to delete or choose whether to delete the Cell Contents or Formulas Only in the current cell. Choose OK.

If you make a mistake, use Edit ➤ Undo (or Ctrl+Z) to fix it.

To Format a Table with the Expert

1. Put the cursor anywhere in the table to be formatted.

2. Choose Table ➤ Expert or click the Table Expert button in the Tables toolbar.

3. In the Available Styles list, highlight the style you want. (A sample table will appear with that style.)

4. If you do not want the style to update if the table size changes, select (check) Apply Style On A Cell By Cell Basis.

5. If you want to clear any current formatting changes before applying the new style, select (check) Clear Current Table Settings Before Applying.

6. If you want to use this style as the default style for all new tables, click the Initial Style button.

7. Choose Apply.

To Format a Table Manually

1. Position the cursor in the cell, column, row, or table you want to reformat, or select the cells, columns, or rows you want.

2. Choose T<u>a</u>ble ➤ F<u>o</u>rmat, press Ctrl+F12, or right-click the table and choose F<u>o</u>rmat from the QuickMenu.

3. Choose how much of the table you want to format: C<u>e</u>ll (includes all selected cells), Co<u>l</u>umn, R<u>o</u>w, or T<u>a</u>ble.

4. Choose Alignment, Appearance, and other options as appropriate from the dialog box that appears.

5. Choose OK.

To Change Table Lines and Shading

1. Select whichever cells contain lines that you want to change.

2. Choose T<u>a</u>ble ➤ <u>L</u>ines/Fill, press Shift+F12, or right-click the table and choose <u>L</u>ines/Fill from the QuickMenu.

3. Choose how much of the table to change (Sele<u>c</u>tion, Each <u>S</u>elected Cell, <u>C</u>ell, or T<u>a</u>ble), as appropriate.

4. Choose from among the various line styles, colors, and fill options to get the look you want.

5. Choose OK to return to the document.

To Delete a Table or Its Contents

Select the entire table (e.g., move the mouse pointer to a line in a table, and when it changes to a vertical or horizontal arrow, triple-click). Then press Delete (Del). Choose from among the following deletion options, then choose OK:

Entire Table   Deletes the entire table, including its contents.

Table Contents   Empties all the cells in the table, but leaves the table structure intact.

Formulas Only   Converts all formulas to their text or numerical results, but does not delete the contents of any cell.

Table Structure (Leave Text)   Deletes the lines and other table codes, but leaves the contents of the table intact. Rows will be separated by hard returns; columns will be separated by [Left Tab] codes.

Convert To Merge Data File   Converts the entire table to merge data file records.

Convert To Merge Data File (First Row Becomes Field Names)   Converts the second row and remaining rows of the table to merge data file records. The first row is converted to field names.

OPTIONS   To create a new Table Expert style that's based on the formatting of the current table, put the cursor in the formatted table, choose Table ➤ Expert, and click the Create button. Enter a unique name for the style, then choose OK and Close.

To delete a Table Expert style that you created, choose Table ➤ Expert, highlight the name of the style to delete in the Available Styles list, then click the Options button, choose Delete, answer Yes to the prompt, and choose Close.

The Options button in the Table Expert also lets you set up, rename, retrieve, and save styles (see *Styles*).

NOTES   Because the Tab and Shift+Tab keys move the cursor from cell to cell, they don't play their normal roles when the cursor is in a table. To tab (indent) within a table cell, press Ctrl+Tab. To insert a back tab, press Ctrl+Shift+Tab.

The QuickMenu and Tables toolbars provide many shortcut alternatives to using the Table menus. To open the QuickMenu, right-click the table. To show the Tables toolbar, activate the toolbar (View ➤ Toolbar), then click in a table.

The order (or precedence) in table formatting is as follows:

Table   Changes made at the Table level affect the entire table, but will be overridden by any other type of formatting.

Row/Column Any formatting changes that you make at the Row or Column level will override formatting changes made at the Table level.

Cell Any formatting changes you make at the Cell level override changes made at the Table, Column, and Row levels.

Other Any changes you make within a table using the regular menus and shortcut keys (such as changing the font) override all of the above. That is, hidden codes within a table cell take precedence over any formatting changes made by going through the Table commands.

 **SEE ALSO** *Columns, Styles, Table Math*

TABLE MATH

WordPerfect tables can be used as spreadsheets, to display numbers, and to perform calculations. If you're familiar with spreadsheet programs, you'll be able to learn the Table Math features quickly.

The Table Math features are easiest to use if you turn on the Table Formula feature bar.

To Display the Table Formula Feature Bar

Choose T<u>a</u>ble ➤ Fo<u>r</u>mula Bar, or click the Formula Bar button in the Tables toolbar. When you're done using the feature bar, click its <u>C</u>lose button.

To Put Numbers into a Table

Type the numbers into their cells in the document window.

To Put a Formula or Function into a Table Cell

1. Select (check) Table ➤ Cell Formula Entry and answer Yes to the prompt. When Cell Formula Entry is selected, Word-Perfect will try to calculate any numbers and formulas that you type into a cell.

2. Move the cursor into the cell where you want the formula, then type in the formula or function (using the correct format and rules for the function).

3. Move the cursor to another cell to see the calculation result.

To resume normal data entry (where numbers and formulas are treated as text and aren't calculated), deselect Table ➤ Cell Formula Entry.

To Enter a Formula or Function Via the Table Formula Feature Bar

1. Turn on the Table Formula feature bar.

2. Move the cursor to the table cell where you want to enter the function or formula.

3. Do one of the following:

   • Type the formula into the Edit Formula text box (using the correct format and rules for the formula or function).

   • To select a function from a dialog box, click the Functions button. If you want to limit the list of functions, choose an option from the List Functions pop-up button (your choices are All, Arithmetic, Calendar, Financial, Logical, Miscellaneous, and Text). Highlight the function you want in the Functions list, choose Insert, then fill in any options required for the formula.

4. Click the Insert (✓) button in the feature bar.

To Point to a Cell or Range

1. Turn on the Table Formula feature bar.

2. In the Formula Entry text box, type all or part of the formula or function that will include the cell or range (if necessary).

3. Position the cursor in the Edit Formula text box where you want the text to appear, or select the text you want to replace.

4. In the document window, click on or select the table cell or range you want, or click on a floating cell in the document window.

5. Finish typing the formula (as necessary), and click the Insert (✓) button in the feature bar.

To Sum a Row or Column

1. Position the cursor at the bottom of the column or at the end of the row of numbers you want to sum. (To sum a row, the cell above the row must either be empty or must contain text.)

2. Click the Sum button in the Table Formula feature bar, or press Ctrl+=, or choose Table ➤ Sum.

To Copy a Table Formula

1. Position the cursor in the cell that contains the formula you want to copy.

2. Click the Copy Formula button in the Table Formula feature bar, or choose Table ➤ Copy Formula.

3. Choose the Destination (To Cell, Down a specified number of times, or to the Right a specified number of times).

4. Choose OK.

You can also use Data Fill (described next) to copy formulas.

To Fill Table Cells with a Formula or Pattern of Data

1. Establish the pattern you want, as follows:

    - *To establish an incrementing pattern* with Roman numerals, days of the week, months of the year, or quarters, type the starting value in the *first* cell of the range. *Examples:* **II** (Roman numeral 2), **Saturday** (day of the week), **February** (month of the year), **Qtr1 or Quarter1** (quarter of the year).

    - *To establish an incrementing pattern of numbers,* or a decrementing pattern of numbers, Roman numerals, days of the week, months of the year, or quarters, type values into the *first two* cells of the range. *Examples:* To increment numbers by 20, starting at 100, type **100** in cell A1 and **120** in cell A2. To decrement the numbers by 20, starting at 100, type **100** in cell A1 and **80** in cell A2.

    - *To repeat a single number, text value, or formula, t*ype the value into the *first* cell of the range. Formula cells will be adjusted automatically, unless you use absolute cell addresses (see Notes, below).

2. Select the cell(s) you entered in step 1, plus any cells that should continue the pattern.

3. Choose T_able ➤ Data _Fill from the menu bar, or press Ctrl+Shift+F12. You can also click the _Data Fill button in the Table Formula feature bar, or right-click the selected cells and choose D_ata Fill from the QuickMenu.

To Recalculate One or More Tables

Do any of the following:

- To calculate the current table or all tables in the document, choose T_able ➤ C_alculate or click the Calculate button in the Tables toolbar, then click _Calc Table or C_alc Document.

Clicking the Calculate button in the Table Formula feature bar will also recalculate all tables in the document.

- To turn automatic calculation on, choose Table ➤ Calculate, and then either Calculate Table or Calculate Document. If you also want to update associated charts whenever you change their source tables, select (check) Update Associated Charts (new in version 6.1). Choose OK.

- To turn automatic calculation off, choose Table ➤ Calculate ➤ Off and choose OK.

To Add a Floating Cell to Your Document

1. Turn on Cell Formula Entry, and display the Table Formula feature bar if you wish.

2. Position the cursor where you want the floating cell to appear (the cursor must be outside of any table or floating cell).

3. Choose Table ➤ Create ➤ Floating Cell, then choose OK.

4. Enter your formula, then move the cursor outside the floating cell (for example, press →).

To edit the floating cell later, turn on Reveal Codes (Alt+F3), move the cursor between the [Flt Cell] paired codes, and make your changes.

NOTES   The intersection of a column and row in a table is called a *cell*. You use cell *addresses* to reference a specific cell in formulas. In cell addresses, columns have letter names (A, B, C, D, and so on), and rows are numbered (1, 2, 3, 4, and so on). For example, the address of the first cell in the table is A1. The address of the cell in the third column and fourth row is C4.

A *range* is a rectangular group cells defined from an upper-left cell to a lower-right cell. Use a colon or period to separate the two cell addresses in a range. For example, B1:C8 or B1.C8 defines the range of cells from B1 (the upper-left cell) to C8 (the lower-right cell).

You can also use *names* to name tables, floating cells, cells, ranges, columns, and rows. Names can be used in formulas and functions, as an alternative to addresses. To create named ranges, and perform other operations on named ranges, choose T<u>a</u>ble ➤ <u>N</u>ames or click the <u>N</u>ames button in the Table Formula feature bar.

A *floating cell* is a formula or number, placed within the document text and enclosed in a pair of [Flt Cell] codes. Floating cells can contain any formulas, text, or numbers that table cells can, and they can reference table cells and other floating cells.

When you copy a formula, its cell addresses are usually adjusted to accommodate the formula's new position in the table. To prevent adjustment of a cell address when you copy formulas, enclose in square brackets the portion of the address that you don't want adjusted. *Examples:* [B]1 (keep the column number constant), B[1] (keep the row number constant), [B1] (keep the entire cell address constant). Cell addresses that can be adjusted during a copy are called *relative addresses.* Those that can't be adjusted are called *absolute addresses.*

When entering the text argument into the formula, enclose the text in double quotation marks. For example, **UPPER ("this is text").**

The QuickMenu and Tables toolbar provide many shortcut alternatives to using the T<u>a</u>ble menu options (see *Tables*).

👁 **SEE ALSO**   *Chart, Tables*

TABS

WordPerfect gives you two ways to set tabs: from the Tab Set dialog box or from the ruler bar. These tab types are available: Left, Center, Right, and Decimal (with or without dot leaders).

To Set Tab Stops with the Ruler Bar

1. Turn on the ruler bar (<u>V</u>iew ➤ <u>R</u>uler Bar or Alt+Shift+F3).

2. Move the cursor to the start of the text where you want to change the tab settings, or select a block of text.

3. Use any method below to add, change, or delete tab settings.

- To *delete a tab stop*, drag the tab marker to below the ruler bar and release the mouse button.

- To *select several tab markers at once*, hold down the Shift key, move the mouse pointer to an empty spot just to the left of the first tab marker you want to select, then drag across the ruler to highlight the tab markers you want to select.

- To *delete several tab markers at once*, select the tab markers, drag the selected tab markers down below the ruler bar, then release the mouse button and the Shift key.

- To *move several tab markers at once*, select the tab markers drag the selected tab markers across the ruler bar to their new position, then release the mouse button and the Shift key.

- To *copy several tab markers to a new position on the ruler bar*, hold down Ctrl and Shift while selecting multiple tab markers. While still pressing Ctrl and Shift, drag the selected tab markers across the ruler bar to their new position, then release the mouse button and the Ctrl and Shift keys.

- To *delete all tab stops*, right-click the bottom of the ruler bar (where the tab markers are) and choose Clear All Tabs from the QuickMenu.

- To *select a tab type* (alignment), right-click the bottom of the ruler bar and select a tab type from the QuickMenu.

- To *set a new tab stop*, select the tab type you want, then click on the ruler bar where you want the new tab to appear.

- To *change the type* of an existing tab stop, delete the tab stop, then set a new tab stop.

- To *move a tab stop*, drag it to a new position on the ruler bar. As you drag the tab marker, the right edge of the status bar will show the exact tab position. *A ruler guide* will also indicate where the tab marker is with respect to the text in your document.

- If, while dragging a tab marker, you want to return the marker to its *original position*, drag the marker above the ruler bar, then release the mouse button.

To Use the Set Tabs Dialog Box

1. Move the cursor to where you want to change the tab settings, or select a block of text.

2. Choose Format ➤ Line ➤ Tab Set to open the Tab Set dialog box. (You can also right-click the ruler bar and choose Tab Set, double-click a tab marker in the ruler bar, or double-click an existing [Tab Set] code in Reveal Codes.)

3. Use any method below to set a tab:

- To *choose how you want to position tabs*, choose either Left Margin (Relative) or Left Edge Of Paper (Absolute).

- To *delete all tab stops*, choose the Clear All button.

- To *delete one tab stop*, choose Position and type the position of the tab stop you want to delete. Then choose the Clear button.

- To *set default tab stops* (left tab stops every one-half inch), choose the Default button.

- To *select a tab type* (alignment), choose a tab type from the Type drop-down list button. Your choices are Left, Center, Right, Decimal, Dot Left, Dot Center, Dot Right, and Dot Decimal.

- To set *equally spaced tab stops*, select the tab type you want to repeat. Choose Position and type in the position for the first tab stop. Select (check) Repeat Every, press Tab, then type the distance you want between tabs. Choose the Set button.

- To *set one tab stop*, select the tab type you want. Choose Position and type in the position for the new tab stop. Make sure Repeat Every is deselected, then choose the Set button.

- To *change the type* of one or more tab stops, follow the procedure above for setting equally-spaced tab stops or one tab stop.

- To *move a tab stop*, delete the tab stop, then set a new tab stop at the spot you want.

4. Choose OK when you're done making changes.

NOTES Use tabs or indents, rather than spaces, to align vertical rows of text or to indent text by a precise amount of space. Tabs are initially set at every 0.5 inches.

Tabs indent to the next tab stop, with text wrapping back to the left margins. Indents temporarily change the left or left and right margins, with text wrapping to the tab stop (see the Indent entry).

Tabs move the cursor to the next cell in tables or to the next level in outlines.

SEE ALSO *Center, Decimal Alignment, Indent, Outline, Styles, Tables*

TEMPLATE

Every new document that you create is formatted according to an underlying template file. Templates establish the initial document text and available abbreviations, toolbars, macros, menus, keyboards, preferences, and styles. (Template features changed between versions 6.0 and 6.1 and the templates in version 6.1 are completely new.)

To Choose a Template When You Create a File

1. Choose File ➤ New, press Ctrl+T, or click the New Document button in the toolbar.

2. In the Group list, highlight or click on the group that contains the template you want.

3. In the Select Template list, highlight the template or template expert you want. (Tip: If an expert is available, try it!)

4. Optionally, choose View to preview the template text.

5. Choose Select.

6. Respond to any prompts that appear.

To Create a Template

1. Choose File ➤ New, press Ctrl+T, or click the New Document button in the toolbar.

2. Choose Options ➤ New Template.

3. Type the text, enter formatting codes, and choose feature bar buttons as needed. (See Options, below.)

4. To save the changes and return to the document window, choose Exit Template from the feature bar and choose Yes when asked about saving your changes. Enter a Description that will appear in the Select Template list of the New Document dialog box, enter a Template Name (one-to-eight characters, with no punctuation or file name extension), and select the Template Group that should contain your new template. Choose OK.

To Edit, Rename, Copy, or Delete a Template

1. Choose File ➤ New, or press Ctrl+T, or click the New Document button in the toolbar.

2. In the Group list, highlight the group that contains the template; then highlight the template in the Select Template list.

3. Choose Options, then do one of the following:

- To edit the template, choose Edit Template and continue with step 3 of the "To Create a Template" procedure above.

- To delete the template, choose Delete Template ➤ Yes.

- To copy the template, choose Copy Template, select the group where you want to put the copy, then choose Copy.

4. Choose Close.

To Create, Rename, or Delete a Template Group

1. Choose File ➤ New, press Ctrl+T, or click the New Document button in the toolbar.

2. If you are renaming or deleting a group, highlight that group in the Group list.

3. Choose Options, then do one of the following:

- To create a new group, choose New Group, type a unique name for the group (one to eight characters, no spaces or punctuation), and choose OK.

- To rename the group, choose Rename Group, type a unique name for the group (one to eight characters, no spaces or punctuation), and choose OK.

- To delete the group, choose Delete Group ➤ Yes.

4. Choose Close.

OPTIONS   These buttons are available on the Template feature bar:

Insert File Retrieves a WordPerfect document at the cursor position. This also will retrieve the document's template objects (keyboards, menus, template macros, toolbars, and styles).

Build Prompts Lets you create prompts and paste placeholders for the answers to those prompts. These prompts (and the user's responses) will appear when a new document is created from the template.

Copy/Remove Object   Lets you copy objects from a specified template to the current template, remove objects from the current template or copy a macro from a disk to the current template.

Associate   Lets you establish a connection between a template object and various WordPerfect modes or features. You can also run (trigger) a macro that's stored with the template when certain events occur. For example, a macro could display some instructions just after you create a new file based on the template.

Description   Lets you change the description for the current template.

Exit Template   Lets you save changes to the template and return to the document window.

NOTES   WordPerfect comes with several built-in templates. The *default* or *standard template* (typically standard.wpt) is used unless you choose a different template via File ➤ New. The *additional objects template* provides an alternative source of objects (keyboards, menus, template macros, toolbars, and styles).

Except for the *main* group, each template group corresponds to a subdirectory of the WordPerfect templates directory (usually c:\office\wpwin\template). The *main* group is the WordPerfect templates directory itself, and it usually contains the standard template (standard.wpt). You cannot delete or rename the main group.

To change the default or additional objects template location, choose Edit ➤ Preferences and double-click File. Choose Templates. Specify the default and additional directory and file names and the default template file extension (usually WPT), as needed. If you want WordPerfect to continually overwrite your default template with the additional objects template, select (check) Update Default Template From Additional Objects Template; this can be handy on a network where the network administrator is maintaining the additional objects template for all to use. Choose OK, then choose Close.

SEE ALSO *Abbreviations, File Management, Initial Codes Style, Macros, Menus, Preferences, Styles, Toolbar*

TEXTART

Use WordPerfect's TextArt feature to add outlines and shadows to text, fill text with patterns and colors, pour text into nearly 50 different shapes, rotate text, and produce other special effects.

To Create a TextArt Graphic

1. Move the cursor to where you want to put the TextArt graphic.

2. Choose Graphics ➤ TextArt, or click the TextArt button in the WordPerfect toolbar.

3. In the text box, type or edit the text that you want to stylize.

4. Use the toolbar buttons, drop-down lists, and menus to choose a font, style, justification, shape, color, outline, shadow, rotation, and any other options as desired.

5. Repeat steps 3 and 4 until you get exactly the look you want.

6. When you're happy with your creation, click on the document window outside the TextArt graphics box. Click outside the box again to deselect it.

To Edit a TextArt Graphic

1. Use one of these techniques:

    *   *To edit in-place* (within the WordPerfect document), double- click the graphic you want to change. Or, right-click the graphic and choose TextArt 2.0 Document Object ➤ Edit. Or, select the graphic and choose Edit ➤ TextArt 2.0 Document Object ➤ Edit.

- *To edit in a separate application window,* right-click the graphic and choose TextArt 2.0 Document Object ➤ Open. Or, select the graphic and choose Edit ➤ TextArt 2.0 Document Object ➤ Open.

2. Repeat steps 3–5 of the above procedure "To Create a Text-Art Graphic."

3. When you're finished, do one of the following:

- If you're editing in-place, click in the WordPerfect document outside the TextArt graphics box, then click outside the box again to deselect the box.

- If you're editing in a separate application window, double-click the TextArt 2.0 window's Control-menu box or press Alt+F4.

OPTIONS Figure 6 shows a TextArt graphics box ready for editing in a separate application window. Notice the menu options, drop-down lists, editing area, toolbar, and sample shapes.

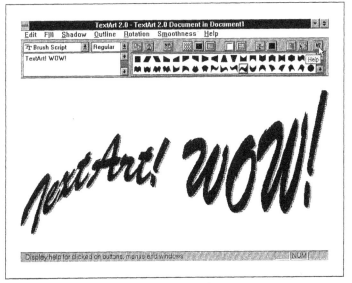

Figure 6: The TextArt application window.

NOTES If you are editing in a separate application window, Help prompts will appear in the status bar whenever you move the mouse pointer to a tool or text box. For more help, click the Help button at the right edge of the toolbar or press Shift+F1, then click the area you're interested in.

The embellished text is placed in a graphics box. You can size and position that box using all the standard techniques described in the Graphics and Graphic Boxes entry.

You can also use WP Draw to curve and embellish text. See the Draw entry.

SEE ALSO *Chart, Draw, Graphics and Graphic Boxes, Object Linking and Embedding*

THESAURUS

Thesaurus lists and substitutes synonyms (words with the same or similar meaning) and antonyms (words with the opposite meaning) for words in your document.

To Look Up a Word

1. Position the cursor on a word you want to look up.

2. Choose Tools ➤ Thesaurus (Alt+F1). If the word you chose is in the Thesaurus, WordPerfect will list words with similar or opposite meanings.

3. To replace the word in your document with a word from the list, highlight the word in the list and choose Replace. To look up a new word, enter the new word in the Word text box, and choose Look Up. To return to your document without changing the original word, choose Close.

OPTIONS

<< and >> Use these buttons to scroll back and forth between lists of words.

Dictionary Lets you specify another Thesaurus dictionary file if you have purchased and installed one.

Edit Lets you cut, copy, and paste between the Word text box and the Clipboard, select all text in the Word text box, and undo your last action in Thesaurus.

History Displays a list of words you have looked up recently.

NOTES The Thesaurus window displays *headwords*, *references*, and *subgroups*. A headword is a word you can look up. References are divided into nouns (n), verbs (v), adjectives (a), and antonyms (ant). References marked with a bullet (•) lead to additional headwords and references. References may be divided into subgroups, which are groups of words that share the same basic meaning.

To look up a reference word marked with a bullet, double-click that word, or highlight it and press ↵. Thesaurus will display the listing for that word in the next available column.

To activate a different column listing, click the mouse on the new column or press ← or →.

To scroll to references *within* a displayed column, use the mouse or the vertical cursor movement keys.

You can also run Thesaurus by double-clicking the Thesaurus icon in the WpWin 6.1 group window in Program Manager.

 **SEE ALSO** *Spell Checker*

TOOLBAR

The toolbars provide shortcut buttons for many WordPerfect operations. WordPerfect comes with over a dozen predefined toolbars. You can customize any toolbar and create new ones. To find out what a button does, move the mouse pointer to the button and read the description in the title bar at the top of the screen. Also look for the QuickTip that appears near the mouse pointer.

To Display or Hide the Toolbar

- Choose View ➤ Toolbar.

You can also hide the toolbar by right-clicking it and choosing Hide Toolbar.

To Select a Toolbar

1. Display the toolbar if it isn't visible (View ➤ Toolbar).

2. Right-click the toolbar and choose the toolbar you want from the QuickMenu.

You can also select a toolbar by choosing Edit ➤ Preferences and double-clicking Toolbar. Highlight the toolbar you want and choose Select, then Close.

To Reposition the Toolbar

1. Display the toolbar if it isn't visible.

2. Move the mouse pointer to a blank area on the toolbar (the pointer changes to a hand icon).

3. Drag the toolbar to where you want it. If you drag the bar somewhere other than the edge of the screen, it becomes a window that you can move and size.

To Change the Appearance of the Toolbar

1. Display the toolbar if it isn't visible.

2. Right-click the toolbar and choose Preferences.

3. Choose Options.

4. Choose the appearance (Text, Picture, or Picture And Text) and Location (Left, Top, Right, Bottom, or Palette for the toolbar.

5. Select the Font Face and Font Size (if you choose Text or Picture And Text in step 4).

6. Choose whether to show QuickTips (if you choose Picture in step 4) and whether to Show Scroll Bar. Specify the Maximun Number of Rows/Columns To Show.

7. Choose OK, then Close.

NOTES   You can add, delete, and move buttons on a toolbar; create new toolbars, and delete existing toolbars. To get started with these operations, right-click the toolbar and choose Preferences. Or choose Edit ➤ Preferences and double-click the Toolbar icon. See *Preferences* for more information.

SEE ALSO   *Feature Bar, Hide Bars, Power Bar, Preferences, Ruler, Status Bar*

TYPESETTING

WordPerfect's Typesetting options include many features used in desktop publishing and typesetting applications. Use them to get precise control over the text in your document.

To Adjust Typesetting Features

1. Move the cursor to where the typesetting options should take effect, or select a block of text (Word/Letterspacing only).

2. Choose Format ➤ Typesetting.

3. Do one of the following:

- To advance text up or down, choose Advance (see the Advance entry).

- To create overstrike characters (characters printed one atop the other), choose Overstrike (see the Overstrike entry).

- To enter special commands for your printer, choose Printer Command and type the command or specify a file name that contains printer commands. If you want to insert a code that pauses printing temporarily, at the cursor position, select Pause Printer. Choose OK.

- To choose word spacing, letterspacing, justification limits, leading adjustments, automatic kerning, and baseline placement for typesetting, choose Word/Letterspacing. See Options, below.

- To kern two letters manually, choose Manual Kerning (see the Kerning entry).

4. Fill in any dialog boxes that appear, then choose OK.

OPTIONS The Word/Letterspacing options are described below:

Normal For word spacing and letterspacing respectively, spaces words or letters according to the specifications set by the font or printer manufacturer.

WordPerfect Optimal Spaces words and letters according to the specifications that WordPerfect considers best.

Percent Of Optimal Lets you specify the spacing width by entering a percentage of the Optimal setting. Percentages greater than 100 increase spacing between words or letters; percentages less than 100 decrease spacing. After selecting a Percent Of Optimal option, you can choose Set Pitch. The Set Pitch options let you specify the pitch in characters per inch (this is converted to a percentage of Optimal). Larger pitches decrease spacing between words or letters; smaller pitches increase it.

Compressed To   Lets you adjust a percentage (0–100) for compressing the spacing between fully-justified words. By default, WordPerfect will compress spacing between fully-justified words to no less than 60 percent of normal.

Expanded To   Lets you adjust a percentage (100–9999) for expanding the spacing between fully-justified words. By default, WordPerfect will expand the spacing between fully-justified words to no more than 400 percent of normal. (1000 or more allows unlimited expansion.)

Adjust Leading   Select (check) this option, then specify the distance you want Between Lines separated by soft and hard returns.

Automatic Kerning   Select (check) this option to reduce excessive white space between certain letter pairs. The pairs of letters that WordPerfect can kern automatically are predefined for each font.

Baseline Placement For Typesetting   When deselected (the default), the *top* of the first line of text is aligned with the top margin. When selected (checked) the *bottom* of the first text line is aligned with the top margin. Selecting this option ensures that the bottom (baseline) of the first text line appears in the same place regardless of font or style.

NOTES   Once a word spacing limit is reached, spacing is adjusted between letters.

To restore settings to the defaults, turn on Reveal Codes (Alt+F3) and delete the appropriate code.

SEE ALSO   *Advance, Codes, Justification, Kerning, Line Height, Line Spacing, Overstrike, Units of Measure*

UNDELETE

The Undelete command restores deleted text (including any codes within that text) at the current cursor position. You can use this feature to move text as well as to restore it to its previous position. WordPerfect remembers the last three deletions, and you can display or restore any one of them.

To Undelete Text

1. Position the cursor where you want to restore the deleted text or codes.

2. Choose Edit ➤ Undelete (Ctrl+Shift+Z).

3. The most recent deletion will appear in reverse video.

4. Do one of the following:

- To restore the highlighted text, choose Restore.
- To display the next oldest deletion, choose Previous.
- To display a more recent deletion, choose Next.
- To return to the document window without restoring, choose Cancel or press Esc.

NOTES While in the document window, you can undelete any of the last three deletions as long as WordPerfect isn't carrying out a command. Use Undelete if you accidentally deleted text or codes, or use it to quickly move or copy previously deleted text or codes.

A *deletion* is any group of characters and codes that you delete *before* moving the cursor to another place in your document.

You cannot undelete paired codes (e.g., [Bold]) deleted with the Delete or Backspace key. However, you can use Edit ➤ Undo or press Ctrl+Z to restore paired codes.

 **SEE ALSO**   *Cancel, Delete, Undo / Redo*

UNDO/REDO

The Undo command reverses the most recent change made to a document. The Redo command reverses your most recent Undo. And the Undo/Redo History feature lets you selectively undo or redo up to 300 changes to your document.

To Undo an Operation

1. Choose Edit ➤ Undo, press Ctrl+Z, or click the Undo button in the WordPerfect toolbar.

2. Optionally, repeat step 1 as needed to undo additional changes, up to the limit specified in Undo/Redo History (see below).

To Redo an Undo

1. Choose Edit ➤ Redo, or press Ctrl+Shift+R, or click the Redo button in the WordPerfect toolbar.

2. Optionally, repeat step 1 as needed to redo additional undos, up to the limit specified in Undo/Redo History (see below).

To Use Undo/Redo History

1. Choose Edit ➤ Undo Redo History.

2. Click on or highlight the operation you want to undo or redo in the appropriate Undo or Redo list. Selecting an item lower in the list automatically selects the items above it.

3. Click the appropriate Undo or Redo button. WordPerfect will undo or redo the selected operations.

4. Repeat steps 2 and 3 as needed. When you're done, choose Close.

OPTIONS To customize WordPerfect's undo and redo behavior, choose Edit ➤ Undo Redo History and click the Options button. Specify the Number Of Undo/Redo Items you want WordPerfect to remember (up to 300). To choose whether to remember recent changes when the file is saved, select (check) or deselect (clear) Save Undo/Redo Items With Document. If you select this option, you can undo or redo changes even after saving and reopening the file (this increases the file's size). If you deselect this option, you cannot undo or redo changes after saving and reopening the file (your file will be smaller).

👁 **SEE ALSO** *Undelete*

UNITS OF MEASURE

WordPerfect uses measurements to position text and graphics on a page. The status bar displays the vertical and horizontal position of the cursor according to the current units of measure. The ruler divisions also reflect the current units of measure.

You can specify measurements in inches, centimeters, millimeters, points, or 1200ths of an inch.

To Change the Default Units of Measure

1. Choose Edit ➤ Preferences and double-click Display.

2. Choose units of measure as follows:

- To set the units for the document window and dialog boxes, choose an option from the Units Of Measure pop-up list button.

- To set the units displayed on the status bar and ruler bar, choose an option from the Status Bar/Ruler Bar Display pop-up list button.

3. Choose OK and Close.

 NOTES Inches are the default unit of measure.

Whenever WordPerfect prompts for a measurement, you can enter either fractions (3½) or decimal numbers (3.5).

WordPerfect uses the default units when you *omit* the units of measure. To temporarily override the default units of measure, *include* the units of measure abbreviation (e.g., **12p** for 12 points). Abbreviations are ″ or *i* (inches), *c* (centimeters), *m* (millimeters), *p* (points), and *1* (1200ths of an inch). The entry will be converted to the default unit of measure.

Although WordPerfect displays up to three numbers to the right of the decimal point, it actually calculates up to six places.

 SEE ALSO *Document Window, Preferences, Ruler, Status Bar*

VIEW

You can view the pages of your document in three ways: Draft, Page, or Two-Page view. You can also edit your document in any of these views.

To Choose a View

1. Choose View.

2. Select one of these options:

- To view the document without page headers, footers, watermarks, footnotes, endnotes, and other page formatting features, choose Draft. (The shortcut key for Draft view is Ctrl+F5.)

- To see a one-page view of the document with all page formatting features, choose Page. (The shortcut key for Page view is Alt+F5.)

- To see a two-page view of the document with all page formatting features, choose Two-Page.

 NOTES There is no Print Preview in version 6 of WordPerfect.

The zoom, ruler, and Reveal Codes features aren't available in Two-Page view.

SEE ALSO *Document Window, Zoom*

WINDOWS

The Window pull-down menu and various buttons and borders on windows let you open, close, size, position, and select windows. WordPerfect for Windows runs in its own *application window*. Each document you edit is in a *document window* (see *Document Window*).

You can use standard Windows techniques and the Window menu to size, position, and switch to various windows. See your Windows documentation for details.

 NOTES The File ➤ Open (Ctrl+O), File ➤ New (Ctrl+T), Shift+F4, and Ctrl+N commands open a new document window. File ➤ Close (Ctrl+F4) closes an active window (see *Save/Save As*).

You must activate (click on) a window before you can edit its contents. The title bar of the current (active) window is usually colored differently from the other (unselected) windows that are also open on the screen.

 **SEE ALSO** *Combine Documents, Dialog Boxes, Document Window, Menus, Save/Save As*

ZOOM

Use Zoom to specify the magnification of on-screen text and graphics.

To Change the Zoom Magnification

Use either of the methods below:

- Choose <u>V</u>iew ➤ <u>Z</u>oom or double-click the Zoom button in the power bar to open the Zoom dialog box. Select a predefined size, or choose <u>O</u>ther and enter a percentage magnification. Choose OK.

- Choose a magnification by clicking the Zoom button in the power bar and then clicking the desired magnification.

To Change the Default Zoom Magnification

1. Choose <u>E</u>dit ➤ Pr<u>e</u>ferences and double-click <u>D</u>isplay.

2. Choose View/<u>Z</u>oom.

3. Select a zoom percentage or enter one in the <u>O</u>ther text box.

4. Choose OK, then choose <u>C</u>lose.

 **SEE ALSO** *Power Bar, Preferences, View*

INDEX

Note: Page numbers in **bold** refer to primary discussions of topics. Page numbers in *italic* refer to illustrations.

Symbols

& (AND) operator, 195
* (asterisk) wildcard, 203
… (ellipsis), in menus, 131
➤ (triangle), in menus, 131
? button (feature bar), 58
? (question mark) wildcard, 203
| (OR) operator, 195

A

abbreviations, **1–3**
  automatic replacement, 171
About WordPerfect (Help
    menu), 83
absolute addresses, 231
active document window, 47
additional objects template, 237
addresses of cells, 230
Adjust Leading, for
    word/letterspacing, 245
Adobe Type Manager, 65
Advance feature, **3–4**, 244
alignment character, changing,
    38
All justification, 104
All Summary Fields
    (QuickFinder dialog box),
    176
Allow Undo, after sort, 192
Alt key, for menu options, 130
anchor options for graphics
    boxes, 75
AND (&) operator, 195
annotating charts, 20
antonyms, 240
appearance of font, 65

Append command, **4–5**
application window, 250
applications, starting at
    specified time, **106–108**
ascending sort order, 194
Associate (Template feature
    bar), 237
associating data file with form
    file, 133
asterisk (*) wildcard, 203
attributes of files, changing, 62,
    148
auto line height, 112, 113
Auto QuickFormat style, 177
Auto Reference Box Captions
    (Create List dialog box), 118
Auto Replace (Spell Checker),
    203
auto replacement words, in
    dictionary, 72
Auto Start (Spell Checker), 203
automatic calculation of tables,
    230
automatic hyphenation, **88–92**
automatic kerning, 245
automatic links, 145
automatic redrawing of charts,
    19
automatic styles, for outlines,
    151, 153
axes in charts, 19

B

Backspace key, 40
  in Typeover mode, 100
backup copies of documents,
    44–45